Hands on Design and Technology

Hilary Ansell

Acknowledgements

I would like to thank all the children from Kingfisher Primary School whose work has been photographed for this book. A big thank you also to the staff for their continuing support. I would like to say a special thank you to Kay Vicars for her great enthusiasm and encouragement.

Thank you also to the staff and children of Woodfield Primary School for their great support and enthusiasm whilst working on the Four Seasons wall hanging and the Fairytale Cottage. I thoroughly enjoyed my time in your school.

Once again, thank you to my friends at St John's Hospice for their interest in my work and their encouragement. Thank you too to my friends Lesley and Sam Young for cups of coffee and afternoons spent brainstorming ideas and a big thank you to John Shanks for his invaluable technical assistance!

The Four Seasons (page 63)

Published by Collins, An imprint of HarperCollins*Publishers*
77 – 85 Fulham Palace Road, Hammersmith, London, W6 8JB

Browse the complete Collins catalogue at
www.collinseducation.com

© HarperCollins*Publishers* Limited 2011
Previously published in 2004 by Folens as 'Starting Points in Design and Technology'
First published in 2004 by Belair Publications

10 9 8 7 6 5 4 3 2 1

ISBN-13 978-0-00-743948-5

Hilary Ansell asserts her moral rights to be identified as the author of this work

British Library Cataloguing in Publication Data
A Catalogue record for this publication is available from the British Library

Every effort has been made to trace copyright holders and to obtain their permission for the use of copyright material. The authors and publishers will gladly receive any information enabling them to rectify any error or omission in subsequent editions.

Commissioning Editor: Zöe Nichols   Editor: Nina Randall
Cover design: Mount Deluxe   Page layout: Suzanne Ward
Photography: Kelvin Freeman   Templates: Celia Hart

Printed and bound by Printing Express Limited, Hong Kong

Mixed Sources
Product group from well-managed forests and other controlled sources
www.fsc.org Cert no. SW-COC-001806
© 1996 Forest Stewardship Council
FSC

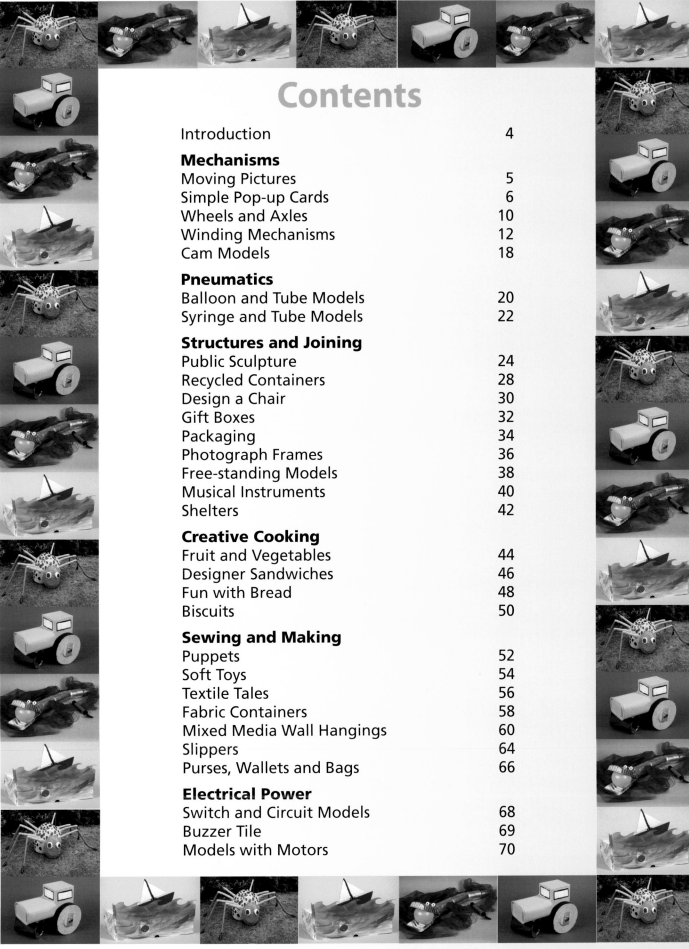

Contents

Introduction

'Where do I start?' This is a question often asked by teachers when faced with the intricacies of teaching Design and Technology to children. 'How do I transform this broad subject into workable activities and provide opportunities for the children to practise and learn the necessary skills?' This book seeks to address these questions.

Hands on Design and Technology is divided into six chapters, each covering a different area of the Design and Technology curriculum. In each chapter, you will find themes that practise the core skills. The activities range from very simple ideas for younger children to more complicated projects for the older pupil. Themes vary between individual, small group, class and whole year group projects. The activities employ many different materials and techniques to produce two- and three-dimensional artwork and models. They range from creating large-scale works of public art to simple pop-up cards and fabric glove puppets. There are opportunities for designing, planning, measuring, marking out, cutting and shaping, joining and combining in a variety of ways. Each theme is set out clearly with easy to follow instructions and is accompanied by one or two full colour photographs, sometimes showing the model before and after it has been finished.

I firmly believe that children have an inherent desire to be creative. They love to make things. Through working independently and with others and by sharing ideas, they can derive great enjoyment and satisfaction.

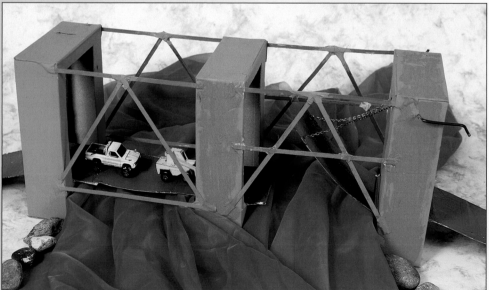

The activities in this book are merely starting points – children should always be encouraged to bring their own thoughts and creativity to each activity and adapt their designs accordingly. Through this process, they will innovate and persevere, and develop a thorough knowledge and understanding of designing and making.

Hilary Ansell

Moving Pictures

Ted in a Bed

Approach

1. Fold a sheet of A4 white card in half. Cut a piece of yellow card slightly smaller than A5. Draw a bed head towards the top of the yellow card. Colour with felt pen. Cut a pillow shape from white card and glue onto the bed head. Draw a quilt shape, roughly 11cm square, on white card and decorate with felt pens.

2. Draw the bed end on card, colour and cut out. Glue this to the lower part of the quilt. Glue along the side edges of the quilt only and position on the yellow card.

3. Draw a bear on white card, colour and cut out. Cut a strip of card long enough to enable the bear to be pushed up and down the bed. Glue the strip to the bear. Slip the bear behind the quilt. Glue the completed picture to the front of the folded A4 white card.

4. Ask the children to design their own pictures using this mechanism. Another example is a 'Frogs on a Log' card made in the same way but replacing teddy's bed with a log shape, glued down only at the ends.

Resources
- A4 white and coloured card
- Felt pens
- Glue sticks
- Paper fastener
- Scissors
- PVA glue

Disappearing Bee

Approach

1. Trim a sheet of blue card slightly smaller than A5. From another piece of blue card, cut a circle 10cm in diameter. Position the circle on the piece of blue card so that part of it overhangs the edge. Very lightly draw round the circle. Cut away a part of the top left-hand quadrant of the lightly drawn circle thus making a window in the card.

2. Make some daisy shapes from white and orange card. Position the wheel behind the window, first pushing the paper fastener through the centre of a daisy and the sheet of blue card. Glue the other daisies in position. Draw a bee on white card. Colour and cut out. Glue this into the window. When the wheel is turned, the bee will disappear. Draw flower stalks in felt pen and cut leaves from green card and glue into position. Mount the picture on a folded sheet of A4 white card.

5

Simple Pop-up Cards

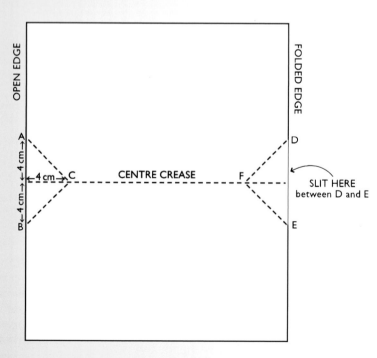

Resources
- A3 cartridge paper
- Coloured paper or very thin card
- Glue sticks
- Felt pens
- Coloured pencils

Approach

1. Fold the paper in half twice to make a card shape. Open up the card and fold the inside crease in the opposite direction.

2. Cut horizontally through the crease. The size of the cut will depend upon the theme of the card. Fold back the edges of the slit to make two right-angled triangles. Turn the card over and fold the triangles over the other way. Do this once or twice to make the creases more workable.

3. Re-fold the card and open out. Pull up the two pop-up pieces and press the pop-up creases firmly. Shut the card with the mouth open and press firmly.

4. Draw a fish, bird or animal head around the open mouth and colour with pens and pencils. Alternatively, cut the creature out of coloured card. Make the mouth exactly the same size, cut away the pop-up pieces from the original card and glue the new mouth/creature over the hole, making sure that the centre folds are exactly aligned.

Surprise Pop-up Cards

Approach

1. Fold a sheet of A3 paper in half twice to make a card shape. Turn the card so that it opens upwards with a horizontal fold.

2. Mark two points on the edge of the paper, one 4cm above the centre fold (A) and the other 4cm below the fold (B). Mark a third point on the fold 4cm from the edge (C). Lightly draw in the triangle.

3. Repeat on the folded edge of the card (D, E and F) and gently slit open the fold between the points D and E.

4. Lightly score along these lines and fold to make half the opening mouth shape (see fish card above).

5. Open the pop-ups out, close the card and press firmly. Cut out and attach hands, arms, wings and so on to these mechanisms as shown on page 7 in the bear and duck cards.

Two-piece Opening Mouth Card

Approach

Resources
- Card
- Ruler
- Scissors
- Glue sticks
- Felt pens

1. The basic mechanism (described at the top of page 6) may be adapted to create any long-nosed creature, such as a fish or crocodile as shown below. First, fold an A4 piece of card in half.

2. Transfer and enlarge the diagram below onto another piece of card 17cm by 10cm. Fold in half lengthways along crease F. Snip open the fold at one end (B) to a depth of about 2cm. Fold the cut ends over at an angle to form tabs (C/D). Trim and discard part E to leave a nose shape.

3. At the tip of the nose (A), fold the last 3cm of the centre crease in the opposite direction and pinch to form two short creases. These will form a 'V' shape for the end of the nose.

4. Repeat steps 2–3 on another piece of card to make the lower part of the jaw but trim slightly smaller.

5. Position the top part of the jaw over the fold of the open card from step 1. Make sure that when the card is folded the nose doesn't stick out. Glue the tabs to the card. Repeat with the lower part of the jaw.

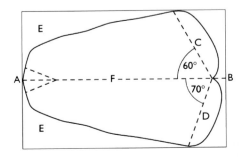

6. Draw the rest of the head around the opening jaws. Fill in the background scene and add detail such as teeth.

Multiple Pop-up Cards

Resources
- Card
- Scissors
- Ruler
- Pencils
- Felt pens
- Glue

Garden Scene

Approach

1. This card uses a similar mechanism to the template on page 7 to create rows of pop-ups. First, fold a sheet of A4 card in half for the base.

2. From another piece of card cut strips 6cm wide and shorter in length than the width of the base card. Fold the strips unequally. Cut open the fold on one side to a depth of 2cm. Fold back the cut ends at an angle as described on page 7, step 2, to make the tabs. Trim the corners off the tabs.

3. Draw motifs or cut them from magazines and glue to the strips of card.

4. Line up the folds of the strips with the centre fold of the base card. Make sure nothing protrudes when the card is folded. Glue the tabs into position.

5. Decorate the base card.

Lucky Ladybird

Approach

1. Fold a stiff piece of green card in half.

2. Cut a piece of red card slightly shorter but a little wider than the green card. Fold this in half and, starting at the folded edge, draw half a ladybird's body and three legs. Hold the folded card together and cut out and decorate the ladybird.

3. Bend the legs to make the ladybird stand up. Bend the ends of the legs under to form tabs for gluing.

4. Fold the ladybird flat and position it inside the card. Glue the tabs on one side. When they are dry, glue the other set of tabs.

5. Open up the card and the ladybird will pop-up. Add a message and decoration.

Platform Pop-up Cards

Resources
- A3 cartridge paper
- Ruler
- Pencils
- Felt pens

Approach

1. Fold an A3 sheet of stiff cartridge paper in half and half again to form a base.

2. Consider how many pop-ups are needed. Three small platforms are plenty for this size card but the children could make one large pop-up.

3. Transfer the diagram below onto the card base. Follow the diagram for cutting and folding. A 2cm high platform is adequate for this scale.

4. Draw motifs or cut shapes from magazines and mount on thin card. Measure the distance between the front edge of the platform and the opening edge of the card. The shapes can be no taller than this otherwise they will show when the card is folded.

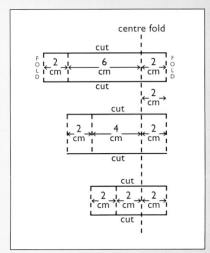

Combine all these various mechanisms to create a pop-up book of a favourite story or perhaps ask the children to write and illustrate their own stories.

Wheels and Axles

Road Roller

Approach

1. To make the roller, pierce a hole in each end of a cylindrical carton. Cut a length of dowel a little wider than the roller and slot this through the holes. Slip beads or washers onto each end of the dowel.

2. Cut a strip of strong card and bend to form a rectangular 'U' that will fit over the roller. Pierce a hole at the centre point of the strip. Push a paper fastener up through the hole. Pierce holes in the 'arms' of the holder and slot onto the dowel. Glue on washers or beads to hold in place. Trim card 'arms' clear of the work surface.

3. Choose a container for the front part of the vehicle, remove one end and pierce a hole for the paper fastener on the roller holder. Fasten the two sections together.

4. Choose a box for the cab and pierce holes to take the axle. Tape or glue the axle into position.

5. To make the large wheels, use ribbon or textile tape reels. Cut strips of thin card and glue between the reel sides. If the hole in the centre of the reel is too large, cover the hole with a card disc and make new holes to fit the axle. Slip the wheels onto the axle, making sure that they spin freely. Glue on washers or beads to prevent them falling off.

6. Tape the front and back sections of the vehicle together ensuring that the wheels and roller run together on the work surface.

7. Paint the vehicle.

Resources
- Wooden, plastic and card wheels in various sizes
- Cotton and ribbon reels
- A large selection of reclaimed packaging materials
- Strong card
- Straws
- Tubing
- Pen casings
- Beads with large holes or washers
- Dowelling of various widths
- Ramin (rectangular dowel)
- PVA glue
- Masking and clear adhesive tape
- Double-sided adhesive tape
- Elastic bands
- Paper fasteners
- Large drawing pins or noticeboard pins
- Simple tools such as a junior hacksaw and bradawl
- Sandpaper
- Wooden clothes pegs

Simple Tipper Truck

Approach

For the body:

1. Discard the lid of a shoebox. With a hole punch or bradawl, pierce holes in the sides of the box to take the axles. Measure carefully to make sure that the holes are aligned so that the axles will be parallel.

2. Cut lengths of thin dowel slightly wider than the box and slip them through the holes, making sure that they turn freely. Slot on the wheels and glue into position with a dab of PVA. Glue on plastic bottle caps as hubcaps.

3. Glue a smaller box into position for the cab and another for the bonnet. Add clear bottle caps as headlights. Cut windows and opening doors.

For the tailgate:

1. Use an open box or ice cream carton for the tipping part of the truck. Cut away the back section below the rim.

2. Cut a length of drinking straw slightly shorter than the width of the box. Tape this along the top edge of the flap.

3. Cut a length of thin dowel the same width as the box. Slip this through the straw, making sure that the ends protrude and that the flap swings easily. Tape the protruding ends of the dowel to the box just below the rim.

4. Tape the open rear edge of the tipping box to the back edge of the truck or fix in place with a card hinge.

5. Paint and then decorate, possibly using cut out computer-generated images and lettering.

Fixed Wheel Truck

Approach

1. Choose a box for the body of the lorry and, using a small hacksaw, cut the ramin to fit the dimensions of the box. Glue the pieces together, adding right-angled triangles cut from card to the corners to give extra strength.

2. Glue four clothes pegs to the underneath of the chassis to hold the axles.

3. Cut dowel axles slightly wider than the chassis. Make sure that the axles will turn freely in the holes of the clothes pegs. Slip the axles through the pegs and fix on the wheels. Glue or pin into position.

4. Glue a smaller box to the body of the vehicle for a cab. Cut around the three sides of the remaining part of the box. Fold this flap down level with the back of the cab. Tape in place.

5. Glue the truck body to the chassis. Decorate as desired.

Winding Mechanisms

Resources
- Card
- Strong thread
- Strong wire
- Plastic or metal tubing
- Clear packaging plastic
- Shoebox
- Beads with holes or washers
- Paper clips
- String
- Adhesive tape
- Paper fasteners
- Glue
- Elastic bands
- Cotton and ribbon wheels
- Dowelling of various widths

Fire Engine

1. Tape lengths of plastic or metal tubing to the underside of a shoebox as axle bearings. Check that the dowelling will turn easily in the tubing and cut it to size. Slip the axles through the tubing and fasten on the wheels.

2. Use a ribbon reel for the turntable. Cut two discs from card the same size as the reel. Glue a disc to one side of the reel. Use a paper fastener to fix the reel to one end of the shoebox lid. Glue the other card disc to the top of the reel.

3. Cut a length of strong card slightly narrower than the diameter of the ribbon reel. Fold this into four and then fold up to create a prism shape. Glue together and then glue to the turntable as a support for the ladder.

4. Cut a length of dowel 6cm wider than the ladder support. Fasten it securely under the top fold of the support. This can be easily done with an elastic band.

5. Cut out two identical ladders from strips of strong card. A quick way to do this is to cut along one side of the strip almost to the top, snip horizontally across the middle part of the strip, cut out every other piece and tape the side strip back into place. If necessary, tape both edges of the strip to strengthen.

6. Push paper fasteners through the top of one ladder and the bottom of the other. Bend the top ones to the front and the bottom ones to the back to create supports for the other ladder.

7. Cut two lengths of strong thread each at least twice as long as the ladders. Put the two ladders together – the ladder with the paper fasteners at the bottom being on top of the other. Tie a thread to each bottom fastener and pass it over the bent pins of the top fasteners.

8. Glue the bottom of the underneath ladder to the ladder support. Tie the ends of the thread to the protruding ends of dowel and tape down. Carefully wind up the excess thread. Keep winding and the ladder will extend.

9. Glue a short length of dowel to the turntable as a handle. Complete by fixing on a smaller box for the cab. Cut out windows and doors, adding clear packaging plastic to the holes.

Working Crane

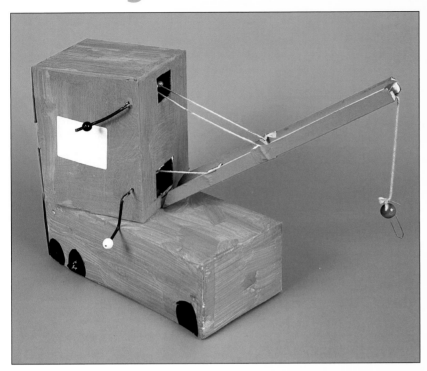

Elastic Band-powered Racing Car

1. Tape two lengths of dowel to a strong cardboard tube to form fixed axles. Slip two cotton reels onto the front axle and two larger wheels onto the rear axle. Use washers or beads for spacers and to stop the wheels from falling off the dowel.

2. Cut a section from a wider card tube, slit and shape to fit around the rear end of the tube chassis. Tape in place.

3. Tape a matchbox to the top of this. Glue the inner of another matchbox to the main tube for a seat.

4. Cut a propeller shape from strong card or plastic. Fasten one end of a flexible piece of wire through the centre of the propeller, slot on a small bead and then a long thin reel or a pen casing. Bend the other end of the wire to form a hook. Tape the reel to the top edge of the matchbox. Squeeze and twist the propeller blades to give a better shape.

5. Hook a strong elastic band onto a strong paper clip. Hook the paper clip over the end of the tube. Hook the other end of the band over the wire protruding from the reel. Turn the propeller to wind up the elastic band. Let it go and the car will move.

6. Experiment with different numbers of bands of various sizes and also different sized propellers.

Approach

1. Cut dowel axles slightly wider than a shoebox. Punch holes near the rim of the open box, push the axles through the holes on one side of the box, slot two cotton bobbins onto each axle and push the end of the dowel through the holes on the other side. Glue or tape the axles so that they do not turn.

2. Cut an upper and lower window in the cab box.

3. Bend two lengths of strong wire to form winding handles, pierce holes in the sides of the cab and slot the winders through the holes so that the wire is accessible through the window. For safety, glue beads to the ends of the wires.

4. To make the crane jib, cut a strip of strong card 6cm by 30cm. Fold over 1.5cm at each long edge. Cut two 30cm lengths of ramin. Cut one end of each length at an angle so that the jib can be raised. Glue the ramin inside the card shape. Trim the card. Tape a piece of card or wire over the ramin to create a channel for the thread.

5. Tape the angled end of the jib securely to the base of the cab, thus creating a hinge so that the jib can be raised and lowered.

6. Tape a long piece of thread to the lower winder and pass it along the channel and over the end of the jib. Weight a paper clip with a bead and tie it onto the end of the thread.

7. Cut two short lengths of thread and secure to the top winder and the jib. Pierce a hole through the chassis box and the base of the cab and join the two together with a paper fastener to make a rotating cab and a fully workable jib.

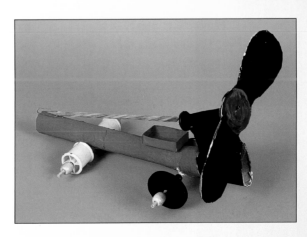

Helicopter

Resources
- Containers of different shapes and sizes
- Adhesive tape
- Pointed pen casing
- Cardboard tubes
- Lightweight cylindrical plastic container
- Washing-up bottle top
- Elastic bands
- Clear plastic packaging

Approach

1. Choose a suitable container for the main body of the helicopter and pierce a hole centrally in the top and the bottom. Position a pointed pen casing between these two holes with the point protruding through the top hole. Tape securely.

2. Cut the propeller blades from a lightweight cylindrical plastic container, leaving the base intact. Punch a hole centrally in the base.

3. Thread a long elastic band through the pen casing. Slip a short length of dowel or a pencil stump through the loop to stop the band from slipping completely into the tube. This also acts as the winder.

4. Onto the other end of the band, thread the upturned top from a washing-up bottle. Now push the band through the hole in the propeller. Cut the end of the band and tape the two pieces to the top of the propeller. Hold the propeller and twist the dowel underneath the container to wind up the band.

5. To complete the body of the helicopter, tape a curved piece of clear plastic packaging to the open end of the container. Tape a cylindrical container to the other end. Glue on short lengths of narrow cardboard tube for the skids.

Windmill

Approach

Resources
- Yoghurt pots of different sizes
- Card or wooden spills
- Glue
- Washing-up bottle top
- Plastic tubing
- Elastic bands
- Matchsticks

1. Pierce a hole in the opposite sides of a small straight-sided yoghurt pot near the base.

2. Cut a length of plastic tubing to fit between the holes. Thread an elastic band through the tube, fit the tube inside the pot and push the ends of the bands out through the holes in the sides of the pot.

3. Thread a bead onto one end of the band and push a matchstick through the loop to prevent the band slipping back into the tube. Thread the top from a washing-up bottle onto the other end of the band. Temporarily secure with a matchstick.

4. Make sails from wooden spills, matchsticks or card. Glue these to a small circle of card. Pierce a hole in the centre of the card and thread the temporarily secured band end through the hole. Thread a matchstick through the loop and tape down so that the band is secured to the card disc. The sails should now turn if the matchstick on the other side is wound. Create the main body from a large yoghurt pot and decorate.

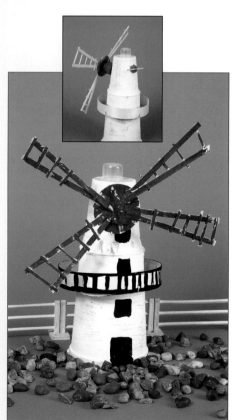

Cotton Bobbin Creatures

Approach

1. Thread an elastic band through a bobbin. Cut the band at one end and tape the two pieces to the end of the bobbin.

2. Cut a 6–8cm length of dowel to act as a brake. Thread this through the band loop at the other side of the bobbin so that a small portion is pushed through the band and the rest drags on the work surface.

3. Wind the band two or three times, let go and see what happens. Try different sized bobbins, bands and brakes. Do plastic bobbins work as well as wooden ones? Try winding more.

4. When the bobbin works well, create a cover from a plastic or paper dish. Cut away a section at one side so that the dish will fit easily over the brake. Decorate the dishes to look like insects or fantasy creatures.

Playground Model

Roundabout

Approach

1. Cut the pointed end off the wooden skewer, making sure that the piece is slightly longer than the pen top.

2. Pierce a hole centrally in the box lid and push the pointed end of the skewer through from underneath, making sure that the pen top will spin freely on the point. Glue the skewer into position.

3. Cut out a circle of strong card the same size as the lid. Pierce a hole centrally in this and insert the pen top. Glue into position.

4. Cut down four bendy straws to form the bars of the roundabout. Glue and tape into position.

5. When the glue is dry, slip the platform of the roundabout over the skewer and spin gently.

6. Decorate as desired.

Resources
- Shallow circular container e.g. wooden cheese box lid
- Wooden skewer or sharpened piece of dowel
- Strong card
- Bendy drinking straws
- Felt pen top
- Glue
- Adhesive tape

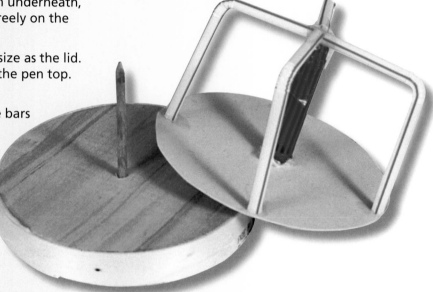

Carousel

Approach

⚠ **Remind the children about safety when using sharp skewers.**

Resources
- Shallow circular container with lid
- Cotton reel
- Empty felt pen casing
- Thin card
- Long elastic band
- Pencil stub
- Adhesive tape
- Drinking straws or thin dowel
- Egg carton
- Thin wire

1. Pierce a hole, large enough to take an elastic band, centrally in the container.

2. Tape a cotton reel centrally over the hole in the upturned container.

3. Make sure that the elastic band will pass through the felt pen casing. Glue the pointed end of the felt pen casing into the hole in the top of the cotton reel.

4. Pierce a hole centrally in the lid of the container

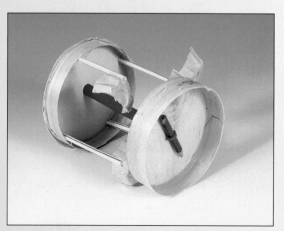

5. Make a hook with the thin wire and using this, pull the elastic band up through the hole in the container, having first secured the other end of the band with the pencil stub, through the cotton reel and pen casing and out through the hole in the lid.

6. Cut the band and securely tape the two ends to the lid.

7. Glue a circle of card to the top of the lid, thus covering up the ends of the band.

8. Cut seats from egg carton cups. Glue to thin dowel or drinking straws and fasten to the inside rim of the lid.

9. When all the glue is dry, twist the pencil stub several times and release to make the carousel spin. Decorate when dry.

Swing

Resources
- Thin wooden dowel or wooden skewers
- Bendy drinking straws wide enough to slip over the dowel
- Glue gun or adhesive tape
- Strong card

Approach

1. Glue two lengths of dowel into an 'A' shape, crossing the tops to create a fork. Repeat this for the other end of the swing.

2. To make the seats, trim the bent end of two straws to a suitable length and insert one into the other, thus creating a 'U' shape.

3. Trim the long straws so that the seat will swing freely when it is hanging from the support. Cut open the ends of the straws and glue or tape around a length of straw slightly wider than the seat.

4. Slip the completed seats over a length of dowel. Glue the dowel into the forks of the 'A' shapes.

5. Brace each end by gluing another length of dowel to the 'A' shape to form a tripod.

6. Decorate when dry.

Cam Models

Clown with Lifting Hat

Resources

- Stiff card
- Foam board
- Prepared cams
- Wooden wheels
- A bead
- Dowelling
- Cardboard boxes
- Rigid metal or plastic tubing
- Drinking straws
- PVA glue
- Masking tape
- Woodworking tools

Approach

1. Draw the clown and a circus scene on the bottom of a shoebox. Cut away the top and shape the card around the clown's head.

2. Drill a hole off-centre in a wooden wheel. The hole must be large enough to take a wooden skewer or thin dowel but fit tightly. Drill another hole in the wheel to take a short piece of dowel for the winding handle.

3. Pierce a hole in the box for the longer length of dowel to pass through. Make sure there is sufficient room to turn the wheel without it catching on the bottom of the box.

4. Tape a length of rigid tubing to the box in line with the centre of the wheel, first making sure that the dowel will pass easily through it. Turn the cam to its lowest position and measure the distance from the top of the cam to the top of the clown's head. Cut a piece of dowel this length. Slip the dowel through the length of tube and glue a small piece of card to the bottom of it to act as a foot.

5. Cut out a hat for the clown and glue this to the other end of the cam follower. Shorten the length of dowel at the front and glue on a bead to stop the dowel from slipping back through the card. Paint the front and back of the model.

Rocking Boat

Approach

1. Drill a hole off-centre in a wooden wheel or shaped cam. Fix a short length of dowel into the hole.

2. Position and glue a cotton reel to the inside of an upturned shoebox.

3. Push the dowel through the reel and through a hole in the side of the box. Drill a hole towards the edge of a smaller wheel and insert a length of dowel long enough to act as a handle. Push this wheel onto the dowel protruding from the box. Cut off any excess. This is the winding handle.

Resources
- Wooden wheels or shaped cams
- Dowelling
- Cotton reels
- Shoeboxes of different sizes
- Ruler
- Rigid tube
- Carton card and wood pieces
- Masking tape
- Large-headed nail

4. Glue or tape a smaller box into the shoebox so that it just touches the side of the cam.

5. Measure the distance between the top of the cam at its highest position and the roof of the box. Cut a length of rigid tube shorter than this distance and tape it to the side of the small box in line with the cam so that the top edge of the tube protrudes slightly through the upturned shoebox. Cut a length of dowel for the cam follower and slip it into the tube.

6. Cut a boat shape from card. Increase the thickness of the hull by gluing several layers together. Attach masking tape along the curved edge of the hull to give a smoother edge.

7. Glue two short pieces of wood together in an 'L' shape to serve as a rigid support for the boat. Use a short large-headed nail to fasten the boat to the support. The boat must pivot smoothly on the nail. Fix the boat so that the end sits directly over the cam follower and drops back with its own weight when the cam follower descends. Glue the boat support to the upturned box. The cam follower should push the curved edge of the boat when it is cranked and the boat should tilt and fall back.

8. Cut a wave pattern along the edge of a strip of card and glue the strip around the top edge of the box. Paint to look like a rough sea and decorate the boat.

Balloon and Tube Models

Yawning Dog

Resources

- Short and long cylindrical containers
- Card tube
- Cotton reels
- Large buttons
- Stiff card
- 2 beads
- Masking tape
- PVA glue
- Balloon
- Balloon pump
- Length of plastic tubing

Approach

1. Glue the cotton reels to the buttons to create legs and paws. Leave to dry.

2. Cut the smaller of the two containers in half from top to bottom. Tape them back together again at one end, having first made a hole large enough for the tubing to pass through. The tape will act as a hinge. Cut card ears and tape into place. Cut two small strips of card. Glue these halfway around the two beads to form the eye casings. Tape them in position in front of the ears. Cut card teeth and tape to the inside of the jaws.

3. Make short cuts around one end of a short card tube. Cut away a section at each side. Bend the sections out. Make longer cuts around the other end of the tube. Tape the shorter sections to the head of the dog, lining up the cut-away sections with the opening jaw. Tape the other end of the tube to the larger container. Cut a card tail and glue in place.

4. When the legs and paws are completely dry, tape them to the body of the dog.

5. Tape the balloon to one end of the plastic tubing. Push the other end of the tube into the mouth, through the neck and body and out through the other end of the dog. Position the balloon in the mouth. Connect the pump to the tube and inflate the balloon. The dog's mouth will open.

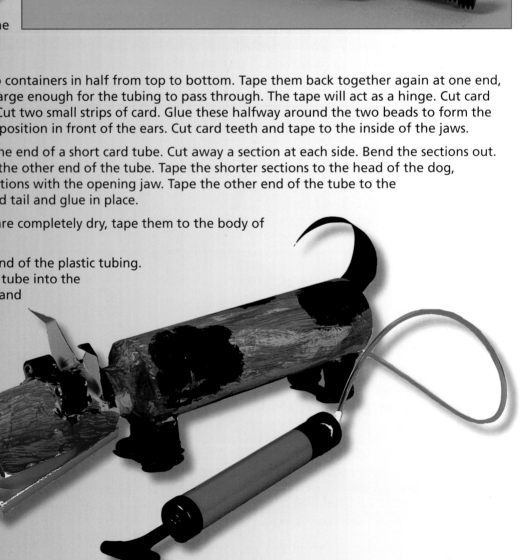

6. Paint or stick fur onto the dog as desired.

Sea Serpent

Resources

- Food trays
- Several large plastic soft drinks bottles or other cylindrical packaging of various sizes
- Cotton reels
- Small piece of fabric
- Masking tape
- Plastic tubing
- Balloon
- Balloon pump

Approach

1. Hinge the food trays together at one end with masking tape to form a mouth. Cut a hole in the lower tray below the hinge large enough to take the tubing.
2. Tape the two cotton reels to the top of the head for eyes.
3. Tape a strip of fabric to the back of the head and around the bottom end of a soft drinks bottle. This will allow movement when the mouth opens.
4. Cut away the bottom from another soft drinks bottle and slot this over the neck of the first bottle. Angle to create a curve in the serpent. Tape securely. Add as many bottles as desired or use other containers, gradually decreasing in size.
5. Tape a balloon to the length of tubing; push the other end of the tubing into the serpent's mouth and out through the hole at the back. Pull the tubing out from under the fabric. Attach the pump, inflate the balloon and the mouth will open.
6. Finish by painting, or cut a length of reptile like fabric or wallpaper and glue this around the body. Alternatively, cut paper scales and cover the whole body with these.

Tipper Truck

Resources

- Shoebox
- Smaller boxes
- Dowel
- Tubing wide enough to take the dowel
- Pre-cut wheels or strong card
- Masking tape
- Balloon
- Plastic tubing
- Balloon pump

Approach

1. Tape the lid securely to the shoebox.
2. Cut lengths of tube for the axle bearings and tape them to the underside of the box.
3. Pierce a hole in the bottom of the box just behind the rear axle bearing.
4. Tape a smaller box to the shoebox lid at the front for the cab.
5. Cut a rectangular hole in the lid behind the cab, leaving enough card all the way round to support the tipping box.
6. Tape the tipping box to the rear edge. The tape acts as a hinge.
7. Tape a balloon to a length of plastic tubing. Push the other end of the tubing out through the hole in the floor of the box. Tape fast. Connect the pump, inflate the balloon and the tipping box will lift.
8. If desired, make a swinging tailgate as described on page 11.
9. Cut windows and doors or simply paint.

Syringe and Tube Models

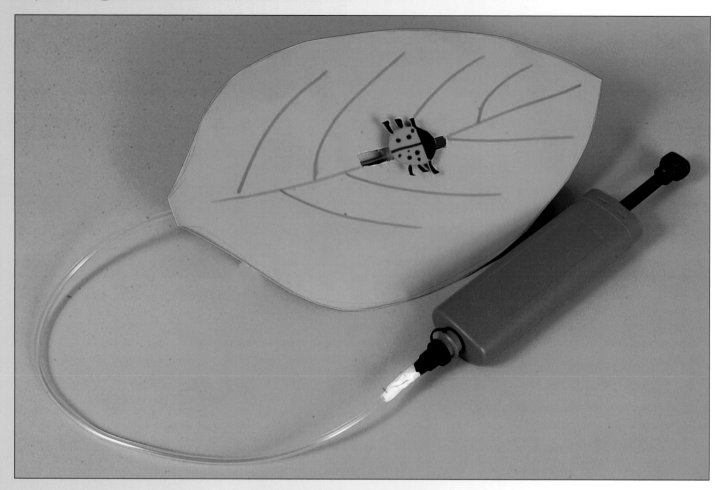

Creeping Ladybird

Resources
- Shoebox lid
- Green and red card
- Masking tape
- Syringes and plastic tubing
- Balloon pump
- Stiff card

Approach

1. Cut away part of the lip of the shoebox lid at one end to accommodate the plastic tube. Tape the syringe to the underside of the lid.

2. Measure the length of the extended syringe plunger. Cut a slot in the lid this length, starting from the end of the syringe with the plunger closed.

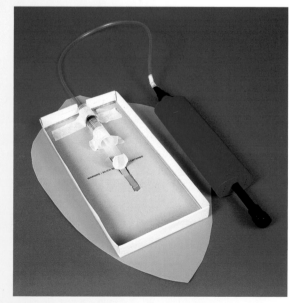

3. Cut a leaf shape from green card large enough to cover the lid. Glue this to the lid and cut out the slot.

4. Draw a ladybird on red card and cut it out. Cut a narrow strip of stiff card, bend it into a right angle and glue one part to the underside of the ladybird and the other to the end of the syringe plunger.

5. Connect the syringe with the plastic tubing and tape the balloon pump to the other end. Push on the balloon pump and the syringe will push along the ladybird.

Pop-eyed Crocodile

Resources
- 2 food trays
- Small box long enough to take the syringes
- 2 small syringes
- Balloon pump
- Connector
- Larger syringe
- Plastic tubing
- Masking tape
- White card
- Pair of tights
- Newspaper
- Vinyl emulsion paint

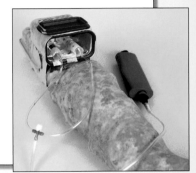

Approach

1. Cut two hinged flaps in one end of the small box. These are the eyelids.

2. Tape the small syringes to the inside of the box behind each eye. Draw eyes on card, cut out and glue to the plunger ends.

3. Tape the two food trays together to form the snout of the creature.

4. Tape the box holding the syringes to the top of the food trays.

5. Cut two lengths of tubing and connect to the syringes. Join the other ends of the tubing to a connector. Add a third length of tubing to the connector and join this to the balloon pump. When the pump is operated, the crocodile's eyes will pop out!

6. To make the body, cut the legs off a pair of tights, pull one leg over the other for strength and stuff firmly with balls of screwed-up newspaper. Attach the body to the head with masking tape.

7. Paint the whole creature with vinyl emulsion paint, as this will adhere to the plastic food trays and the tights fabric. Whilst wet, mottle with ready-mixed paint in a different shade of green.

Apple Tree

Approach

Resources
- Carton card
- Small box
- Syringes
- Balloon pump
- Tubing
- Adhesive pads
- Masking tape
- Paper fasteners
- Invisible sewing thread
- Wire
- Pebbles

1. Cut a tree from carton card. Glue this to the small box. Weight the box with pebbles so that the tree is stable.

2. Cut a strip of card. Fasten a short length of thread to one end of the strip. Cut out an apple from the red card and attach to the other end of the thread. Fix the strip behind the tree canopy with the paper fastener so that the apple is hidden from view.

3. Attach a short length of wire to the other end of the strip. Connect the syringe, tubing and balloon pump together. Tape the other end of the wire to the plunger of the syringe. Tape the syringe to the tree.

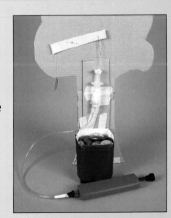

4. Weight the apple so that when the syringe is operated, it will lower smoothly.

5. Complete the tree with more cut-out apples and fix with the adhesive pads to give the tree a slightly three-dimensional appearance.

Public Sculpture

Paper and Plastic Trees

Resources
- Long carpet tubes
- Newspapers
- Coloured plastic bags
- Large umbrella
- Masking tape
- Adhesive tape
- PVA glue
- Plastic-coated garden wire
- Paint
- Varnish
- A post

Approach

1. Look at the different shapes of trees. Listen to the wind rustling the leaves. Think of the scale of trees and ask the children to consider how they could recreate these elements.

2. Tape three carpet tubes together with masking tape to create a wide tree trunk.

3. Twist sheets of newspaper into paper 'ropes'. Using PVA, glue these all over the tree trunk to create a textured bark. Tape the ends of the ropes to the carpet tubes to hold them in position whilst the glue dries, otherwise they tend to unwind.

4. When the glue is dry, paint the trunk in the desired colours using acrylic paint or household emulsion. Add several coats of varnish if desired.

5. To make the tree canopy, first make a hoop of plastic-coated garden wire the same circumference as the umbrella. Carefully remove the fabric from the umbrella. The ribs of the umbrella will now swing about. To prevent this, use thin wire or tape to fasten the tips of the ribs to the hoop.

6. Cut brightly coloured plastic bags into long narrow strips and tie or tape them along the ribs of the umbrella and around the circumference. Slot the handle of the umbrella into the space at the top of the tree trunk and tape securely into position.

7. Hammer a post into the ground outside and slot the construction over this to ensure a stable structure.

Plastic and Cane Shrubs

Resources
- Plaster of Paris
- Garden canes
- Green plastic bags
- A bucket or large plant pot

Approach

1. Line the pot with a plastic bag. Mix up the plaster according to the manufacturer's instructions and pour some into the plastic bag. When the plaster starts to set, push in several garden canes to create a conical structure.

2. When the plaster is completely set, remove the structure from the container. Cut green plastic bags into long narrow strips and weave around the framework until it is completely covered.

3. Display the shrubs outside and attach a handful of plastic streamers to the top to flutter in the wind.

Wire and Tin Can Trees

Approach

Resources
- Large catering cans
- Strong plastic-coated garden wire
- Thin wire
- Metal bottle tops
- Plastic tape
- A stake

1. Remove both ends from all the tin cans except one. Only remove one end from this. Using strong plastic tape, join the cans together to form a tall open-ended metal pipe, leaving out the one-ended can.

2. Use a hammer and nail to make holes in the top of the remaining can. Cut lengths of plastic-coated garden wire to the required length to use as 'branches'.

3. Using a hammer and nail, punch holes into metal bottle tops and wire these to the 'branches' as leaves.

4. Slot one end of the 'branch' through a hole in the top of the can and use pliers to curl the end of the wire around to prevent it slipping out of the can. Repeat this process until the tree canopy is complete. Finally, tape the canopy in place on top of the tree trunk.

5. Display the tree slotted onto a stake outside.

Giant Fantasy Insects

Approach

Basic Structure

1. Before starting the project, thoroughly research the subject of insects, asking the children to make sketches of body shapes and parts. Next, as a class, use a knitting needle or something similar as an aid to roll up a plentiful supply of paper spills. Fasten each spill with masking tape.

2. To create the body, use masking tape to fasten some of the spills together to form hoops. To add extra strength to the structure, cut lengths of plastic-coated garden wire and tape these into hoops. These form the rib cage of the creature. Join the ribs together with long paper spills and masking tape, alternating paper and wire ribs.

3. When the basic structure is complete, carefully stuff it with scrunched-up newspaper.

4. Cover the whole structure with pasted pieces of newspaper. Time permitting, allow to dry between layers. Make necessary adjustments to the shape as work progresses. Add sufficient layers to create a strong structure.

5. To make the head, interlock several spill hoops to create a sphere. Repeat steps 2 and 3.

6. When head and body are dry, tape together with masking tape and join with layers of pasted paper.

Resources

- Knitting needle
- Newspapers
- Plastic-coated garden wire
- Masking tape
- Cellulose paste
- Household vinyl emulsion
- Chicken wire
- Coloured tissue paper
- PVA glue
- Varnish
- Yoghurt pots

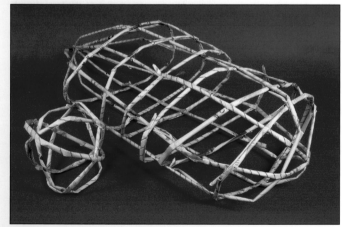

7. To make the insect's legs, tape several spills together to the required thickness and length. Bend to form a knee joint. Wind around with long strips of pasted paper. Leave to dry.

8. Using a craft knife, cut small holes in the sides of the insect and insert the legs. Tape into position and strengthen the join with layers of pasted paper. Insert the ends of the legs into black plastic film canisters and tape securely to the body.

9. Tape yoghurt pots or similar small containers into position for the eyes. Cover with strips of paper. When dry, paint the insects with vinyl emulsion. Add several coats of varnish if the structure is going to stand outside.

Wings

1. Wearing protective gloves, cut wing shapes from chicken wire. Bend any protruding pieces of wire over to create a smoother, safer edge.

2. Using diluted PVA glue for strength, glue pieces of tissue paper over both sides of the wing. Wrap around the edges. Add several layers. Varnish when dry.

3. Supporting the wings on the knees of the insect, tape them into position with wide clear tape.

Recycled Containers

Resources
- Aluminium soft drinks cans
- Round pencil or short length of dowel
- Craft scissors
- Glue gun

Soft Drinks Can Nightlight

Approach

1. Pierce a hole below the top edge of the can at the point where the side becomes very thin. Carefully cut away the can top.

2. Make vertical cuts almost down to the bottom of the can about a centimetre apart.

3. Curl each metal strip outwards around a pencil or piece of dowel. Curl the whole strip.

4. Repeat the process with another can.

5. Glue one curled can inside another. Place a nightlight inside and use as a garden light.

Variations

- Stack several curled cans, one inside the other. Quite a tall construction can be made in this way.

- Turn the holder upside down so that it rests on the curls and place the candle on the concave base.

- Cut petal shapes rather than vertical slits. Curl gently.

- Turn the curled cans into flowers. Hammer a hole in the base of the can. Push a length of strong wire through the hole from the back. Use pliers to curl the end of the wire so that it doesn't slip back through the hole. Bend the wire behind the flower head so that the head cannot slip down the stem. Place the flowers in a large vase or push into a flower bed outside!

Customise a Carrier Bag

Approach

Resources
- Stiff plastic or paper carrier bags
- Coloured plastic carrier bags of any kind
- Clear adhesive tape

1. Flatten and smooth out a stiff carrier bag. Fold in half from the bottom. From the folded edge, cut vertically through back and front at 3cm intervals. These are the warp strips. Do not cut through the reinforced top edge or the bottom of the bag. Open out the bag.

2. For the weft, cut similar sized plastic bags into 3cm wide strips (wider if really flimsy bags). Make sure that the strips are long enough to weave all the way around the carrier bag. Start to weave under and over the strips on one side of the bag. Complete this side first, pushing the weft strips down firmly to create a strong weaving.

3. Turn the bag over and repeat the process on the other side.

4. To finish off, neaten and tuck each end under a warp strip. Secure with clear tape.

Recycle a Glass Jar

Resources
- Jam or sauce jars
- Galvanised wire
- String
- Garden twine
- Coloured synthetic twine
- Buttons with shanks
- Beads
- Sequins
- Corks
- Masking tape
- Wire cutters
- Round nosed pliers
- Large-eyed knitter's needle

 This activity needs close adult supervision. Remind the children to take great care when handling glass. Younger children should use clear plastic containers instead.

Approach

1. Cut four lengths of wire slightly longer than twice the height of the jar.

2. Bend a wire across the bottom of the jar and up the sides. Hold in place with masking tape near the neck of the jar. Repeat with the other wires, crossing them over each other on the bottom of the jar.

3. Use the pliers to curl over the protruding ends of the wires.

4. Thread up the needle with a length of string. Tie the other end to the crossed wires on the bottom of the jar, thus holding them all together. Working in a spiral, wrap the string around each wire in turn. Depending on whether the children go under or over the wire first, they will make a ridged or smooth pattern.

5. Once the wrapping has progressed up the jar a little way, thread buttons, beads and slices of cork or sequins onto the string as it is wound around the jar.

6. If using as a candle or nightlight holder, leave sections of the jar unwrapped, otherwise work to the top, gradually removing the masking tape. Pull the wires tightly to the neck of the jar with the last rows of wrapping and finish off. Use as a vase or storage container for buttons and beads.

Design a Chair

Look at a range of manufactured chairs with the children and identify the materials that have been used in their construction, for example wood, metal, plastic, fabric and so on. How does the chair stand up? What holds it together? Is it comfortable? Does it look good? Look at the work of furniture designers past and present. Some designers have made chairs out of surprising materials, such as glass and paper. Are the children's chairs going to be functional or 'a work of art'?

Plastic Bottle Spindle Chair

Resources
- A large number of interestingly shaped plastic bottles
- Carton card
- Masking tape
- PVA or glue gun
- Paint and other materials with which to decorate the finished model
- Strong card tube

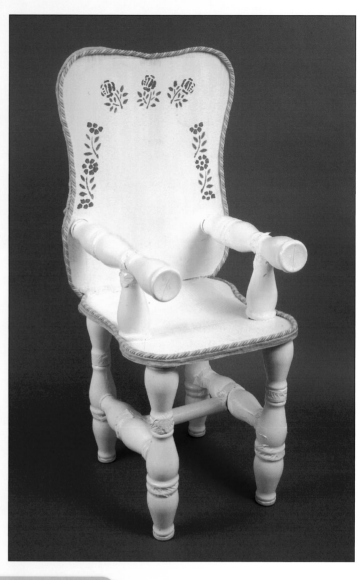

Approach

1. Experiment with ways of putting the bottles together to create the desired shape of the spindles. The children might need to glue two or three bottles together. Construct four legs and two side spindles.

2. Glue the side spindles between the pairs of legs. A glue gun gives instant adhesion here but PVA glue and masking tape will work.

3. Create a central brace from a strong card tube cut to fit around the curves of the side spindles. Tape or glue into position. The structure will now stand upright.

4. Measure the seat area and cut a shape from carton card. Use this as a template to cut three or four more seat pieces. Glue all the pieces together with PVA to make a strong seat. Glue this to the legs.

5. Create arms and arm supports by taping or gluing together more bottles.

6. Make a chair back from layers of carton card. Glue to the back edge of the seat. Glue the chair arms into place.

7. Paint and decorate when completely dry.

Tin Can and Wire Chair

Resources
- Tin cans, washed and with tops safely removed
- Chicken wire
- Strong cardboard tubes
- Silver duck tape
- Newspapers
- PVA glue
- Decorator's brushes
- Paint

Approach

1. Tape the cans together to form the legs of the chair. Brace the legs with lengths of cardboard tubing. Fasten between the cans with duck tape.

2. Cut a length of chicken wire long enough to form the chair seat and back. Curl each end over into a roll. Bend the sides under so that there are no sharp edges. Bend the length of wire so that it forms a seat and a chair back. Crease at this point. The wire will flop back again but it will be easier to fold again when the paper has been applied.

3. Using a decorator's brush for swiftness, brush complete sheets of newspaper with PVA and apply to both sides of the chicken wire. Wrap sheets around the edges of the wire. Apply several layers for strength. Bend the wire back into a chair shape, prop up and allow to dry. The glue and paper will set in this position.

4. Twist two sheets of newspaper into a rope. Brush another sheet with PVA and roll the 'rope' up in this and squeeze together. Tape the dry ends to the chair back and seat to form an arm and stop the back flopping backwards. Repeat for the other side. Glue layers of paper over the joins. Leave to dry.

5. Prop the chair upside down and tape the legs into position. Glue layers of newspaper around the join and leave to dry.

6. If the chair is top heavy and falls backwards, remove the bottom can from the front two legs and add a little sand or gravel before taping back together.

7. Paint or spray silver.

⚠ **Always spray in a well-ventilated space and wear a protective mask. This is best done by an adult.**

Gift Boxes

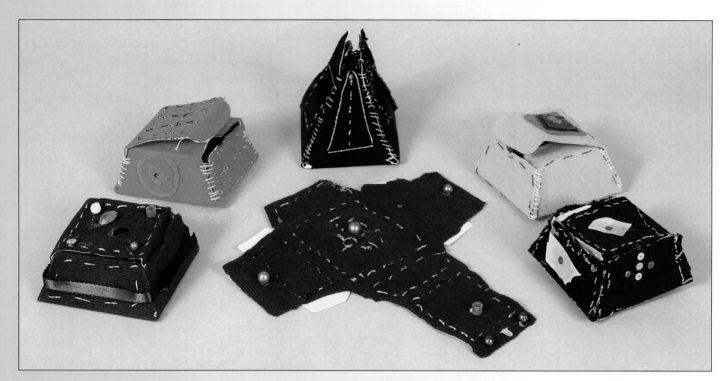

Before starting the project, allow the children to handle some solid shapes and consider how they could reproduce a shape in card and develop it into a container. Count the number of faces and edges. Take apart some small boxes to examine how they are constructed. Note the use of tabs.

Approach

1. On squared paper, draw a net of the gift box, remembering to add tabs for securing. Use the templates on the next page as a guide. Cut out and fold to ensure that the net works.

2. Draw around the flattened pattern on thin card. Carefully mark in all the fold lines. Cut out and fold to ensure that the card shape works.

3. Flatten the card net. Fold the 'joining tabs' up out of the way and glue the net to a piece of felt, making sure that all the edges are glued well. Use the glue sparingly. The stitching will hold the card and fabric together. Do not soak the card. Allow the glue to dry before stitching.

4. Decorate the stiffened net with simple embroidery stitches. A simple running stitch in glittery thread is very effective. Pass a contrasting thread under the running stitch. Outline the faces of the net with stitching. Add sequins or cut shapes from contrasting coloured felt and glue to the faces of the box.

Resources
- Solid shapes
- Examples of small card containers
- A3 squared paper
- Thin white or coloured card
- Felt
- Embroidery threads
- Latex fabric glue
- PVA glue
- Sequins
- Thin, coloured paper or tissue

5. At this stage, the net could be lined with thin coloured paper or tissue to disguise the underside of the stitching but this is not always necessary.

6. Fold the net again, making sure that the creases are as sharp as possible. Glue together.

7. For extra strength, oversew the joined edges of the box, only stitching through the felt.

Variations

- Use iron-on interfacing to strengthen the box instead of thin card.

- Use printed fabrics instead of felt but seal the edges of the lid with PVA to prevent fraying.

- Take apart manufactured tissue boxes and use the nets to create slightly larger boxes to use as covers for other tissue boxes.

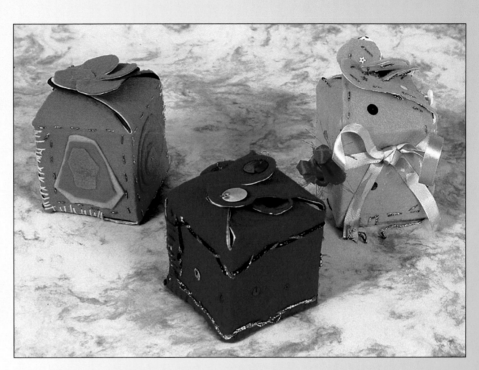

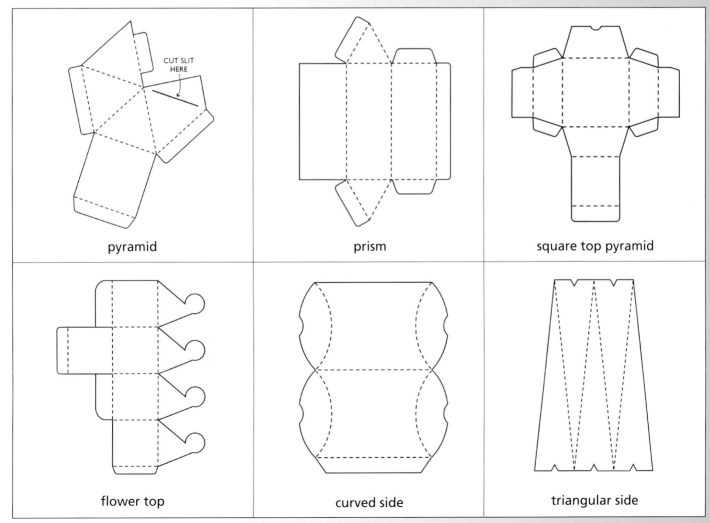

pyramid	prism	square top pyramid
flower top	curved side	triangular side

(pyramid net labelled: CUT SLIT HERE)

Packaging

Cylindrical Packaging

Resources
- Sheets of thin card
- Transparent packaging plastic
- Clear adhesive tape
- PVA glue
- Glue sticks
- Paper clips
- Paint
- A pair of compasses
- Ruler
- Scissors
- Tissue paper

Approach

1. To make the base of the box and a platform on which to stand the toy, measure the overall width of the toy and add 2cm. Draw a circle of this diameter on thin card. Add 2cm to the radius and draw another circle around this. Cut out the large circle. Snip at regular intervals around the circle, cutting up to the line of the inner circle. Fold the flaps down. Decide how deep the base platform is to be (this depends on the overall height of the packaging) and cut a strip of card slightly longer than the circumference of the base. Glue this around the base. Secure with paper clips until the glue dries.

2. Measure and draw the rectangle that is to form the main body of the box, remembering to add an overlap. Draw an oval shape for the window. At this point, customise the box for the particular toy – a tree for an owl, a rocket for a space bug. Draw the top part of the tree or rocket so that it extends above the top line of the rectangle. Cut out the whole shape. Cut out the hole for the display window. Paint before assembling.

3. Tape a piece of transparent plastic behind the window and glue the card around the base. Hold in place with paper clips. Seal the join at the back with clear tape.

4. Make the lid as for the base but only 2 or 3cm deep. Remember to add an opening/closing tab. Paint.

5. Choose appropriate font styles and print out the name of the toy and relevant information. Glue this to the box.

6. Put the toy in the box and slip a piece of yellow card behind it to enhance the display. If the toy wobbles about, add crumpled tissue paper to stabilise it.

Cuboid Packaging

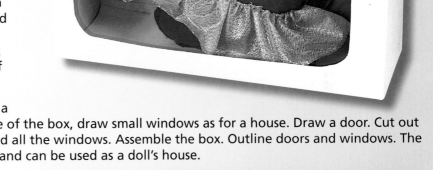

Approach

1. Before starting this activity, make sure that the children have had plenty of practice at disassembling cuboid packaging and drawing nets.

2. Measure the overall height, width and depth of the toy. On squared paper, starting in the centre with the base of the box, draw the net, remembering to add on tabs and a top with a fold down flap. On the top edge opposite the opening flap, draw a roof shape complete with chimney stack.

3. Cut out the net and draw around this on card, remembering to mark in all the fold lines, flaps and tabs. Cut out the card shape. Score the fold lines. Fold to check that everything fits. Make adjustments if necessary.

4. Open out and on one of the sides, draw a large viewing window. On the other side of the box, draw small windows as for a house. Draw a door. Cut out all the windows. Tape clear plastic behind all the windows. Assemble the box. Outline doors and windows. The box is dual purpose. It packages the toy and can be used as a doll's house.

Design a Carrier Bag

Resources
- Stiff white paper
- Printed wrapping paper
- Card
- Felt pens
- String

Approach

1. Younger children could be given an enlarged version of the template below but older children could design their own nets for a carrier bag. Transfer the template onto white paper and mark in all the fold lines.

2. Cut card-reinforcing strips for the top. Fold down the top of the bag; insert the strips and glue together. Fold the bottom section of the bag to the inside. Make all the vertical and diagonal folds and the bag should assemble easily.

3. Before gluing the bag together, open it out and draw on the design. Glue the bag together and reinforce the base with a piece of loose card.

4. Punch holes in the top and thread with string. Laminating a sheet of wrapping paper or the white paper can make an extra strong bag.

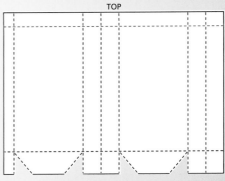

TOP

Photograph Frames

Resources
- Carton card
- Wrapping paper
- Thin card
- Wool
- Raffene/artificial straw
- Buttons
- Paint
- PVA glue
- Paper clips

Cat Frame

Ask the children to examine different types of commercially made frames and identify how they are able to stand up. Discuss the ways of making a piece of carton card stand up. Consider ways of folding and stiffening paper or thinner card to create supports for the frame. Design a frame for an existing photograph or create the frame, then scan a photograph and modify it to fit the frame.

Approach

1. Cut a rectangle from carton card. Draw lightly around this on another larger piece of card. To the top edge of this outline, add the shape of a cat face. Cut out the whole shape. Cut out a separate tail shape. Using a craft knife and a safety ruler, cut a rectangular hole in the centre of the shaped piece.

2. Apply a line of PVA glue around three sides of the rectangular shaped piece of card, leaving the fourth side unglued so that the photograph may be slipped in. Glue this behind the cat shaped piece. Paper clips will help hold the two pieces together until the glue is dry.

3. Cut out a tongue from card and glue into position. Glue short lengths of wool over the cat face. Glue on buttons for eyes and a nose. Glue the end of the tail behind the frame and cover the rest with wool.

4. Cut a length of carton card slightly narrower and longer than the frame. Score, fold and secure this to create a free-standing triangular shape. Glue this to the back of the photo frame.

Bird's Nest Frame

Approach

1. Cut out two identical nest shapes. Cut a hole in one. Glue the pieces together around the edges leaving a section unglued for the insertion of the photograph.

2. Paint the frame and glue on lengths of play straw. Make papier-mâché eggs and glue onto the frame.

3. To make a support, cut a rectangle of stiff card slightly shorter than the frame and about a third of the width. Make zigzag folds in a smaller piece of card and glue one end of this to the bottom edge of the rectangular support and the other end to the frame. Glue the top edge of the support to the frame.

4. For other frames (such as the ladybird as shown) follow the basic method as described above, but for the supports, cut two right-angled triangles from thick card. Score 2cm in from the vertical side and fold to create a lip. Glue the triangular supports to the back of the frame.

Resources
- Self-hardening modelling material
- Wire
- Round-nosed pliers
- Thin dowel or pencil
- Paint
- Varnish (optional)
- Play straw

Clay and Wire Photo Holders

Approach

1. Choose a theme and model the appropriate shape.

2. Cut a length of wire and twist one end several times around a piece of dowel or a pencil to create a coil.

3. Slip the wire off the dowel and flatten the coil, squeezing the rings together as much as possible. Push the other end of the wire into the model. Leave to dry thoroughly and then paint.

4. Varnishing will create a good finish but this must be done in a well-ventilated area.

Free-standing Models

Elephant

Resources
- Strong carton card or wood
- Newspapers
- Cellulose paste
- Thin white paper or white household emulsion
- Paint fabric
- Coloured plastic bags
- Masking tape
- Off-cuts of timber
- Hinges
- Screws

Approach

1. Prepare a large elephant base shape cut from wood or several layers of strong carton card glued together for strength.

2. Roll a large number of newspaper spills and secure the ends with masking tape (see page 26). Tape the spills together until they are long enough to curve from the top edge of the elephant to the belly edge. Tape a line of curving spills vertically across the body. Weave other spills in and out of these horizontally until a basket-like framework has been made. Tape down all the ends.

3. Fill the framework with crumpled sheets of newspaper. For less deep areas, such as the legs and head, tightly scrunch up sheets of newspaper and glue onto the baseboard with PVA. Keep adding scrunched-up paper until the required depth is achieved. Cover the whole structure with several layers of pasted newspaper. The more layers that are added, the stronger the structure will be.

4. Cut an ear from carton card. Bend the card a few times to make it supple. Add shape with twists of newspaper. Tape the ear into position and paste a layer of white paper over the whole shape or simply paint with white emulsion to cover up the newsprint. When dry, paint over again in the desired colour. Cut out a head covering and saddle-cloth from brightly coloured fabric and decorate.

5. For the back support: If carton card has been used for the baseboard, make three-dimensional triangular supports from carton card and glue to the back of the shape. If wood has been used, a hinged support can be constructed from timber off-cuts and screwed to the back.

Bridge with Simple Winding Mechanism

Approach

1. Draw identical rectangles on the back and front of three boxes. Using a craft knife, cut around the two vertical sides and top of each rectangle. Score the bottom edge and open out the flaps.

2. On two of the boxes, fold one of the flaps back through the hole, leaving a small projection of about 3cm. Line up the boxes and tape the long flap of one box onto the short projection of the other. The remaining flap forms the run up to the bridge.

3. Brace the two boxes with art straws, strips of card or wooden spills.

4. The final box forms the drawbridge. Tape a piece of strong card over the space between the two flaps, making a hinge with the masking tape at one side so that the flap can be raised.

5. Bend the wire to form a handle and support for the chains. Push this through one side of the box just below the top of the arch. Wire the length of chain onto the support and push it through the other side of the box. Bend the end of the wire so that it cannot slip out.

6. Make holes in the end of the drawbridge and push the ends of the chain through, adjusting to the correct length. Tape any excess chain under the flap to act as a weight to hold the bridge down.

7. Brace this box to the other bridge piece, aligning the drawbridge flap with the short projection on the other box.

8. Paint the completed model. The bridge can be made with any number of spans. Older children should be able to make a double drawbridge with calibrated action so that the two sections open at the same time.

Resources

- Strong, same sized cardboard boxes (detergent cartons)
- Strong card
- Masking tape
- A length of strong wire
- Short length of thin flexible wire
- A length of fine chain (broken necklace)
- Art straws or wooden spills
- Craft knife
- Safety ruler
- Paint

Musical Instruments

Cow Bells

Resources
- Tin cans of all sizes with one end safely removed
- Metal washers
- Nails
- Screws
- Nuts and bolts
- Wooden beads
- Hammer
- Thin wire
- Wire cutters
- Electrical tape
- Acrylic paints

Approach

1. Pierce a hole in the centre of the upturned can using a hammer and nail.

2. Cut a length of wire long enough to pass through the can and double over to make a handle.

3. Push both ends of the wire through the hole in the top of the can. Fasten a metal washer, nut or bolt to one end of the wire. Adjust the length of the wire so that the washer hits the rim of the can. Twist the other end around the length holding the washer to form a knot and prevent the can from slipping down the wire. Pull the loop up to form the handle. Bind with tape.

4. Squash the tin at the bottom edge to give more of a bell shape.

5. Use acrylic paints to decorate with mountain scenes or alpine flowers.

6. Try using a wooden bead or other things as the bell clapper. Discuss with the children how the sound changes. Does the size of the tin affect the sound? Does the sound change if the clapper is hung higher in the tin?

Beaded Drum

Resources
- Drum shaped lidded container
- Wooden beads
- Thin string or coloured garden twine
- Coloured card
- Glue
- Tapestry needle
- Hand drill

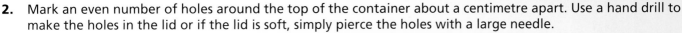

Approach

1. Draw around the container lid on coloured card, decorate and cut out the circle.

2. Mark an even number of holes around the top of the container about a centimetre apart. Use a hand drill to make the holes in the lid or if the lid is soft, simply pierce the holes with a large needle.

3. Thread the tapestry needle with a length of string at least twice the height of the container and tie a bead or button onto the end of the string. Thread the string with beads or buttons until the strand is as deep as the container. Stitch down through one hole in the lid and up through the next. Add more beads to make the next strand. Make sure that the end bead is securely fastened. Repeat until all the holes have been used.

4. Make sure that all the strands of beads are hanging evenly around the container and glue the coloured card circle to the lid, making sure that it is well stuck down over the string.

Bottle Button Shaker

Approach

Resources
- 1-litre soft drinks bottle
- Buttons
- Thin string or garden twine
- Adhesive tape
- Wide dowel or broom handle to fit the bottle opening
- Poster paint
- Glue

1. Mix glue with poster paint and drip into the bottle. Twist the bottle around to create coloured streaks all around the sides.

2. While this is drying, thread up strands of buttons slightly over twice the length of the bottle. Thread up and down the holes in the buttons so that the buttons lie edge to edge. Leave a space halfway along the string so that the strand of buttons can be taped to the bottom of the upturned bottle.

3. Completely cover the sides of the bottle with strands of buttons so that they overlap slightly and knock against each other. Make sure that the end buttons are fastened on very securely.

4. Tie the ends of the strands to the neck of the bottle so that they don't become tangled when the bottle is shaken.

5. Cut a length of dowel for a handle and secure into the neck of the bottle.

Shelters

Hexagonal Summerhouse

Resources
- Newspapers
- Carton card
- A pair of compasses
- Knitting needle
- Narrow adhesive tape
- PVA glue

Approach

1. This basic method may be used to construct a whole range of shelters, from bus stops to log cabins. Use the compasses to mark out a large hexagon on carton card. Draw another hexagon 3cm larger around this. Cut out the large hexagon.

2. At each corner, cut to the inner line. Score the lines of the smaller hexagon and turn down the 3cm strips, trimming the excess from the corners so that the edges of the 3cm strips fit together to form a dais or base. Tape together.

3. Use the knitting needle to roll up a plentiful supply of newspaper spills (see page 26). Tape the spills at intervals along their length so that when they are cut they will not spring apart.

4. Cut six 35cm lengths of paper spill. Tape these to the base at each point of the hexagon. Brace these supports about halfway up with short lengths of spill. Tape in place. Remember to leave one open for the door. Divide the bottom sections diagonally with more short lengths of spill for added strength. The structure should be quite firm now. Join the tops of the supports all the way around.

5. Divide the top of the construction in half with a roof beam. Decide upon the pitch of the roof and bend and tape lengths of spill to form three right-angled triangles. These are the main roof supports. Tape into position and add three more short lengths to complete the hexagonal roof shape.

6. Fill in the bottom half of the construction with lengths of spill, gluing them to the base and the horizontal bar.

7. Measure the triangular roof shapes (quite possibly these will be different sizes) and cut triangles of carton card. Glue into place. Cut a small circle of card, slit to the centre and pull around to form a cone for the roof.

8. Paint the model when completely dry.

Log Cabin

Approach

1. Follow the basic method as before but start with a large rectangle.

2. Tape on two supports at each corner, one on each face of the base. Position two supports at the centre front of the cabin a little way apart for the door supports. Add extra supports on the other sides. Add horizontal and diagonal supports as before. Join all the support tops with more spills. Make four 'A' frames to support the roof. Strengthen the 'A' frames with central vertical supports. Tape into position.

3. Join all the 'A' frame points together with a long paper spill.

4. Fill in the framework by gluing on lengths of spill. Leave spaces for the windows.

Gazebo

Resources
- Thin dowel
- Bendy drinking straws
- Stiff card
- Adhesive tape
- Plastic bags or old shower curtain
- Flexible clear plastic
- Sewing cotton
- PVA glue

Approach

1. Decide upon the scale and measurements of the gazebo.

2. Construct three same sized rectangles or squares using the bendy joints of the straws and lengths of dowel. Slip the dowel into the ends of the shortened straws and secure with tape.

3. Hold the corners of the rectangles steady by gluing on small right-angled triangles cut from stiff card.

4. When dry, tape the three rectangles together to form the three sides of the gazebo.

5. Measure the diagonal of the rectangle or square and then construct four right-angled triangles using half this measurement as the length of the triangles' base. These four triangles form the supports for the roof. Tape the four uprights together and then tape the structure to the sides of the gazebo.

6. Measure the triangular faces of the roof shape, checking for differences. Cut four pieces of waterproof fabric this size, remembering to add on a little extra for seams. Stitch together to form a roof cover.

7. Cut four fabric pieces for the sides. Cut a window hole in one side. Sew or glue clear plastic over the hole. Sew the gazebo side pieces to the bottom edges of the roof cover. Add small string ties so that the sides can be rolled up in fine weather!

Fruit and Vegetables

Potato Hedgehogs

Always stress to the children the importance of good hygiene when cooking. Ensure the children have washed their hands and covered their clothes with an apron prior to cooking. Before starting, revise the safe use of equipment, such as knives, and point out the equipment that can only be used under adult supervision, such as the food processor or cooker.

 Always check with parents for food allergies before involving children in the handling of ingredients.

Our hedgehogs are made from mashed potatoes, milk, butter, cheese, carrots, peas and cherry tomatoes

Potato Hedgehogs

 Approach

1. Wash and peel the potatoes, cut into smaller pieces and put on to boil.

2. While the potatoes are cooking, wash, peel and slice the carrots. If you are adding bacon to the recipe, snip it into small pieces and fry in its own fat. Grate the cheese. Shell the peas and put them on to cook.

3. When the potatoes are ready, drain and mash, adding a knob of butter and a little milk and seasoning. Add the grated cheese and bacon.

Resources
- Potatoes
- Carrots
- Peas
- Milk
- Butter
- Cheese (optional)
- Bacon (optional)
- Seasoning
- Small cherry tomatoes
- Vegetable peeler and knife
- Saucepan
- Potato masher

4. Shape quantities of mashed potato into hedgehog shapes, either as individual portions, or create one large hedgehog on a serving plate. Use the strips of carrot as spikes. Use the tomatoes as noses and peas for eyes. Surround the hedgehog with a ring of peas for a lawn!

Spreads and Dips

Spreads and dips can be easily made using a food processor. Have available a variety of ingredients for the children to choose from to create their own recipes. Talk about which ingredients might go together to produce a tasty spread. Have a taste test after the children have made the spreads.

Approach

1. Blend all the ingredients together until they form a thick paste. Use straight away or store overnight in the refrigerator in an airtight container.

Suggested Combinations

- Carrot, onion, egg and mayonnaise
- Cucumber, cream cheese and spring onion
- Pear, raisin and pineapple
- Pineapple, honey and sunflower seeds

Resources
- A grater
- A blender or food processor
- A rubber spatula
- Juicer (optional)
- Variety of ingredients including fresh fruit and vegetables

Smoothies

Approach

1. Have available a wide range of fruit, including packets of frozen berries. The latter will give a wonderful colour to the drinks. The children might find vegetables such as carrot, tomato and cucumber acceptable but also encourage them to experiment with others, such as beetroot, watercress, celery and lettuce.

2. It is useful to have a juicer as well as a blender as some children do not like the thicker consistency of the blended drinks. If you are not using a juicer, grate harder fruit and vegetables before adding to the blender.

3. Make a fizzy drink with the addition of sparkling water.

4. Smoothies are juices made with the addition of dairy milk, coconut milk, yoghurt or ice cream. Add honey as a sweetener if necessary.

Resources
- A grater
- A blender or food processor
- A rubber spatula
- Juicer (optional)
- Variety of ingredients including fresh fruit and vegetables

Suggested Combinations

- Apples and carrot
- Carrot, cucumber and beetroot
- Apple, melon, red grapes and a little lemon juice
- Strawberries, banana and orange

Designer Sandwiches

Down on the Farm

Resources
- Sliced white bread, white with added grain, granary and wholemeal bread
- Animal and fish shape cutters
- A variety of sandwich fillings
- Low fat spread, mayonnaise, salad cream, tomato sauce
- Kitchen foil
- White and coloured card
- Felt pens or coloured pencils

Approach

1. This simple idea presents the food and the shape together. Cut shapes from a variety of sliced breads. If the appropriate cutter is not available, draw the shape on card, cut it out and use as a template.

2. Encourage the children to select a filling to match the sandwich, for example sliced beef and dairy products, such as cheese spread, grated cheese and cream cheese for a cow shaped sandwich.

3. When filling the 'fish' sandwiches, combine the tuna or salmon with mayonnaise to help it stick to the bread. Also include a few vegetarian options.

4. Cut out plate sized shapes from card. Cover the fish shape with kitchen foil. Colour the shape if the appropriate coloured card is not available. Laminate the plates and arrange the sandwiches on top.

 Check with parents for religious and dietary restrictions.

Sandwich Wheels

Approach

1. Encourage the children to design their own sandwich fillings and collect the ingredients together.

2. Cut the crusts off the slices of bread; thinly cover with low fat spread and the chosen filling. Secure the roll with a cocktail stick.

3. Carefully cut some of the rolls into shorter lengths, securing each section with a stick. The cross section looks like a Swiss roll.

Resources
- A variety of sliced breads and fillings that will roll up easily, such as spreads, cheese slices, Edam or cream cheese, grilled sausages, marmite, marmalade
- Low fat spread
- Cocktail sticks
- Coloured card and kitchen foil
- Cling film

Wraps and Pockets

Vegetable Fajitas

Resources
- 1 tablespoon of olive oil
- 1 large sliced onion
- Crushed garlic clove (optional)
- 1 red and 1 green pepper thinly sliced
- 125g sliced button mushrooms
- 1 teaspoon of chopped oregano
- Seasoning
- 6 tortillas
- Cocktail sticks

Vegetable Fajitas
Ingredients
Tablespoon olive oil, 1 large sliced onion, crushed garlic clove (optional), 1 red and 1 green pepper thinly sliced, 125g sliced button mushrooms, teaspoon chopped oregano, seasoning, 6 tortillas, cocktail sticks

How to make:
- Fry the sliced onion and garlic in a frying pan until soft and golden. Ask an adult to help you first.
- Add the sliced peppers, and oregano and stir. Fry gently for another 10 minutes until the vegetables are cooked.
- Add the sliced mushrooms, stir thoroughly and cook for another minute. Add salt and pepper.
- Warm the tortillas in an oven-ask an adult to help you. Spoon the mixture onto the warmed tortillas, fold up the bottom and fold the sides across. Hold together with a cocktail stick. Alternatively fold in both sides and roll up the tortilla.

Encourage the children to design their own fillings and collect the ingredients together. Below is the basic recipe, which can be adapted easily by alternating the types of vegetable used.

Approach

1. Fry the sliced onion and garlic until soft and golden.

2. Add the sliced peppers and oregano. Fry gently for another ten minutes until tender.

3. Add the sliced mushrooms, stir thoroughly and cook for another minute. Season to taste.

4. Spoon the mixture onto the warmed tortillas, fold up the bottom and fold the sides across. Hold together with a cocktail stick. Alternatively, fold in both sides and roll up the tortilla.

Sausage and Bacon Wraps

Resources
- Streaky bacon
- Pork sausages
- Tortillas
- Selection of sauces (tomato, brown and barbecue)
- Tomatoes
- Lettuce

grated apple and cheese pocket

sausage and bacon wraps

We designed sandwiches using different types of bread.

egg and pickle pocket

Approach

1. Grill several rashers of streaky bacon and pork sausages, drain on kitchen paper and then cut into small pieces.

2. Spoon onto warm tortillas with a little sauce.

3. Add a little chopped tomato and shredded lettuce and roll up the tortillas.

If cooking facilities are not available, try filling pita bread pockets with some of the following cold ideas.

- Mix chopped cucumber and spring onion with tuna mayonnaise.
- Mix grated apple and cheese with a little mayonnaise.
- Fill the pocket with a favourite salad combination.
- Chop a hard-boiled egg and mash with a little pickle.

Fun with Bread

For best results, use a strong plain flour which, when kneaded, will develop quickly into firm elastic dough. Fresh or dried yeast can be used. Fresh yeast can be stored in a cold place for four or five days. Dried yeast will keep for up to six months if stored in an airtight container. Allow two level teaspoons of dried yeast for every 15g of fresh yeast recommended in a recipe. To reconstitute dried yeast, warm a little of the measured liquid, dissolve in this a teaspoon of sugar and sprinkle the yeast on top. Leave for about ten minutes until frothy and add to the rest of the dry ingredients with the remainder of the warmed liquid.

Kneading and Rising

After mixing, knead the dough thoroughly for at least ten minutes. All yeast doughs need to be left to rise at least once to allow the yeast to work. Always cover the bowl with a damp cloth or cling film during rising to prevent a skin from forming on the dough.

Animal Shapes

Approach

1. Prepare the bread dough following a standard recipe and knead thoroughly.

2. Divide the dough into smaller portions and shape into animals.

3. Place the animal shapes onto lightly greased baking trays, making sure that they are well spaced out to allow for rising.

4. Cover the trays loosely with cling film and leave in a warm place until the shapes have doubled in size. Uncover, brush lightly with the beaten egg and bake on the top shelf of a pre-heated oven. Refer to the original recipe for timings and temperature.

Resources
- Wholemeal or mixed grain bread flour
- Dried or fresh yeast
- Warm water
- Mixing bowl
- Fork
- Baking trays
- Scissors
- Teaspoon
- Skewer
- Cling film
- 1 egg, beaten
- Raisins

Hedgehogs
To form the spikes, cut small 'V' shaped cuts all over the back of the hedgehog. As the dough rises, these will open out and give a spiky appearance. Use a skewer to make holes for the eyes or add raisins.

Crocodile
Make a cut in the blunt end of the shape for the mouth. Form two small balls of dough and fix onto the top of the head with water. For a scaly appearance, cut with scissors or press the end of a teaspoon into the dough to create a repeated pattern.

Cobra
Roll the dough into a long shape that is thicker at one end. Coil up from the thin end, brushing with a little water to fix the shape together. Make a slit in the thick end for the mouth and use a skewer to make eyeholes.

Snail
Make a small pointed sausage shape for the body. Roll a longer shape, brush lightly with water and roll it up. Fix the coil to the body with water.

Greek Plait

This is a Greek variation on the country plait and incorporates an egg. The eggs are dyed red and baked in the Easter loaves as a symbol of rebirth.

Resources
- A quantity of white bread dough
- Hard-boiled, white-shelled eggs
- Red food colouring
- 1 beaten egg
- Poppy seeds
- Lightly greased baking tray

Approach

1. To colour the eggs, place them in a pan of cold water containing plenty of food colouring, bring to the boil and simmer gently for about 30 minutes.

2. For each plait, divide the dough into three equal portions. Roll each portion into a long sausage shape.

3. Moisten one end of each sausage with water and press all three ends firmly together. Plait the 'sausages' loosely, incorporating the now-cooled egg into the plait. Moisten the ends of the 'sausages' and press together firmly.

4. Place the plait on a greased baking tray, brush lightly with the beaten egg and sprinkle over with poppy seeds.

5. Leave to rise until doubled in size and bake according to the recipe.

Fruity Whirls

Approach

Resources
- A quantity of sweet yeast dough
- Currants, chopped dates, peeled sliced apple, sweet mincemeat
- Sugar
- Dried fruit salad
- Melted margarine
- Rolling pin
- Lightly greased baking trays
- 30ml milk

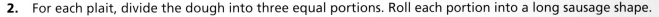

1. Divide the dough into portions. Roll each portion into an oblong and brush with melted margarine.

2. Sprinkle with sugar and add the chosen filling. There is no need to sprinkle with sugar before adding the sweet mincemeat.

3. Roll up the oblong as if making a Swiss roll. Moisten along the edge with water and press to the roll to stop it uncurling when sliced.

4. Slice the fruity 'sausage' into thick slices and lay the slices on a greased baking tray. Leave to rise in a warm place until doubled in size.

5. Bake in a hot oven, gas mark 7 or 220°C for 15 to 20 minutes or until golden brown. Whilst they are still hot, brush with a sugar glaze.

Sugar Glaze
Place 30ml of milk, 30ml of water and two 15ml spoons of sugar into a saucepan. Heat gently until the sugar dissolves and then boil for two minutes. Brush the glaze over the whirls while they are hot.

Biscuits

'Let's Celebrate'

Approach

1. Sift flour and any spices into a bowl. Chop the butter into pieces and rub in until the mixture resembles fine breadcrumbs. Add the sugar and any other dry ingredients. Mix to a very stiff dough with beaten egg.

2. Turn out onto a floured board and knead gently until the dough is smooth. At this point, if time allows, the dough could be put into a polythene bag and left to chill in the refrigerator for 30 minutes to make it easier to roll. However, if the dough is firm and not sticky, roll it out to about 0.5cm thickness and cut with the shape cutters. Alternatively, draw shapes on firm card, cut out, place on the dough and cut around with a sharp knife.

3. Place the biscuits on greased baking trays and prick well with a fork. Bake in the centre of a preheated oven for about 12 to 15 minutes (or until pale gold) on gas mark 4 or 180°C. If you wish to hang any of the biscuits as decorations, make a hole at the top of each biscuit with a skewer immediately after they come out of the oven. Leave the biscuits until firm and then cool off on wire racks.

4. Decorate trees with green fondant icing or marzipan. Roll out the icing and cut out tree shapes to fit the biscuits. Decorate with gold and silver cake decorations. Thread narrow coloured ribbon through biscuits with holes. Wrap others in cellophane and tie with ribbon or package (see page 34) in coloured card.

Resources

- 225g self-raising flour (or use half plain white and half plain wholemeal flour)
- 150g butter
- 140g caster sugar (or use soft brown sugar)
- Beaten egg to mix
- Spices
- Fondant icing
- Marzipan
- Food colourings
- Cake decorations
- Shape cutters
- Firm card
- Narrow ribbon
- Cellophane

Resources

- 125g soft margarine
- 125g soft brown sugar
- 1 small egg, beaten
- Cake decorations
- 175g sifted plain flour
- 50g ground almonds
- Icing sugar, food colourings

Alphabet Fun

Approach

1. Cream the margarine and sugar together until light and fluffy. Mix in the egg, stirring thoroughly.

2. Stir in the flour and almonds a little at a time until the mixture forms a firm dough. Divide the dough and roll out into 1–2cm thick sausage shapes. Cut into shorter lengths, place on greased baking sheets and bend to form letter shapes.

3. Bake in a preheated oven, gas mark 4 (180°C) for 15 minutes or until pale gold. Decorate with coloured icing and cake decorations when cold.

Savoury Bites

Resources
- 150g self-raising, plain and wholemeal flour
- 75g grated mature cheddar cheese
- 75g butter or margarine
- Milk
- $\frac{1}{4}$ teaspoon salt
- $\frac{1}{2}$ teaspoon mustard powder
- 1 small egg
- Crushed potato crisps
- Poppy, sesame and celery seeds
- Walnut pieces and pecan nuts are useful for flavouring or decoration
- A variety of spices and herbs

Approach

1. Sieve together flour and dry flavourings and seasoning. Chop up the margarine and rub into the flour until the mixture resembles fine breadcrumbs.

2. Mix in the grated cheese (crushed crisps could also be added at this point). Add sufficient beaten egg to make a stiff dough.

3. Roll out thinly. Shape as desired with cutters or by cutting into strips. Tie the strips into knots, leave straight or twist.

4. Bake at gas mark 4 or 180°C for 10 to 15 minutes.

Variations

- Roll out the dough into an oblong. Spread half with marmite, sprinkle on a little grated cheese, fold over the other half and press down lightly. Cut into shapes or fingers.

- Use half white and half wholemeal flour. Replace the cheese with $\frac{3}{4}$–1 teaspoon of curry powder and a tablespoon of sesame seeds.

- Add finely chopped fried bacon to the basic recipe with the cheese. Cut into rounds rather than straws.

Puppets with Gussets

Approach

1. To create a pattern for the front and back of the puppet, draw around the hand (fingers closed) on a piece of paper. Enlarge and extend this shape to create a closed 'U', which will extend past the wrist.

2. Using the paper pattern, cut out a front and back from non-fraying fabric. Cut the rounded end off the paper pattern and use this to cut out two gusset pieces in felt for the mouth.

3. Using a backstitch, sew the two gusset pieces together along the straight edge (back of the mouth). With supervision, older children could use a sewing machine.

4. Placing right sides together and matching the curves of the mouth, sew the back and front pieces to the mouth gussets. Complete by joining the straight side edges of the back and front. Turn the right way out.

5. Cut eyes from felt and either sew on or fix into position with fabric glue.

Resources
- Fabrics such as felt, fleece and fur fabric
- Sewing thread
- Toy filler
- Fabric glue
- A4 paper
- Chunky wool
- Sewing machine
- Needles

This basic pattern may be adapted to create a variety of puppets. To create a puppet able to 'swallow', leave the centre of the back of the mouth seam unsewn.

Horse To the basic puppet, add felt ears, nostrils and a mane of chunky knitting wool. Make a small carrot by sewing a triangle of orange felt and a few snippets of green together. Feed this to the horse through the gap in the back of its mouth.

Cow Depending on the type of cow, sew white patches onto black background. Add felt ears and nostrils. Draw a fat crescent shape on paper and cut out to use as a pattern for the horns. Cut two pieces from white felt. Sew around with tiny stitches, leaving a small space through which to stuff the toy filler. Sew up the gap and sew into place between the ears. If desired, sew on a tuft of chunky wool to hang over the centre of the horns like a fringe. For 'grass', cut a small rectangle of green felt. Snip along one edge to create a fringe. Roll this up and secure with a stitch or glue. Feed the grass to the cow!

Blackbird When cutting the pattern, give the mouth end a more pointed shape. Now cut the pattern in two, thus creating a beak/head and a body piece. Cut the gussets to match the beak pieces. Cut all four beak pieces from yellow felt and the body from black. Sew one beak piece to the front body and another to the back. Complete as before. Cut a double wing shape from black felt (extra feathers may be added) and position across the body. Sew into place. The wings should flap up and down with the movements of the hand. Make a worm out of felt or a chenille pipe cleaner.

Puppets without Gussets

Approach

1. Draw around the hand, thumb and little finger outstretched, the remaining three close together. Adapt this shape to create a pattern with a head and two arms/finger spaces. Extend the pattern to cover the wrist. The pattern may now be used as it is to create simple same-coloured puppets to illustrate stories such as the 'Three Little Pigs' (with the addition of eyes, ears and snout) or the 'Three Bears' (cut pattern from fur fabric).

2. The pattern may be divided into pieces to create more complicated characters such as Goldilocks or other male/female characters. Cut the pieces from different coloured fabric, allowing extra for seams, and reassemble. With right sides together, sew the front to the back and turn the right way out. Add hair, features, hats and so on.

Soft Toys

Cartoon Style Spiders

Approach

1. Use a template or draw around a large circular object. Cut out a circle of brown or black fabric and, using double thread, sew all around the edge of the circle with small running stitches. Once back to the beginning, pull up the thread so that the circle puckers up and creates a 'bag'. Fill this firmly with toy filler. Pull the thread firmly to close up the 'bag'. Stitch securely.

2. Cut long, thin rectangles of fabric for the legs. Twist together pipe cleaners to the required length. Fold the fabric legs around the pipe cleaners and oversew. Sew the legs to the underside of the spider. Bend to look realistic.

3. Add expression with eyes and mouth cut from felt.

4. Make smaller spiders in the same way but use coloured pipe cleaners for the legs. Sew sheering elastic to the tops of the small spiders and display them around the large spider.

Variations

Octopus: Make as for the spider but use a pale, smooth fabric.

Crab: Do not fill as firmly. Flatten the shape into more of an oval. Sew the legs around the sides of the shape. Slit the ends to look like claws.

Resources
- Fabrics such as felt, fur fabric, plain and printed cottons
- Toy filler
- Sewing threads
- Fabric glue
- Bobble craft eyes

Toys Using Two Circles

1. Use fur fabric and cut one circle slightly smaller than the other. Gather and stuff both. Sew the smaller to the larger for a head. The joins of both circles should be together.

2. Add felt features such as eyes, arms, wings and feet.

3. Use different fabrics to create cats, rabbits, birds and bears. Make in different sizes to create families such as the 'Three Bears'. Create a fantasy or space creature using a mixture of metallic, sparkly and fur fabrics in bright colours.

Toys from Flat Circles

The simplest way to make a soft toy is to sew together and stuff two flat shapes. If felt is used, the sewing can be done on the right side and there is no need for turning. The circle may be modified slightly to make the shape more oval. It may be cut in half to provide body and head sections, which can then be cut from different colours.

Approach

1. Ask the children to design characters based on a circle, adding arms, legs, hair, hats, collars, ties, belts and so on. Make full sized pattern pieces.

2. Cut the arms, hands, legs and feet sections double; sew and stuff lightly.

3. Slip these between the front and back body pieces and pin in position. Sew around the shape, leaving a gap for stuffing. Stuff and sew up the gap.

4. Cut features from felt and glue into position.

5. Cut lengths of wool for hair. Unravelled knitting gives a lovely curly effect. Try plaits with ribbons or short spiky tufts.

6. Add finishing touches such as buttons and braid.

Textile Tales

Jason and the Golden Fleece

Resources

- Large piece of background fabric (medium weight calico or cotton sheeting)
- Scraps of fabric in greens and greys
- An old velvet curtain (or similar from a charity shop)
- Blue shiny fabric
- Green plastic bags
- Brown wools
- Hessian
- Weaving sticks
- Polyester toy filler
- Latex fabric glue
- Sewing machine
- Felt pen

Approach

1. Read the story with the class. Ask the children to decide which elements to illustrate in the hanging.

2. Identify the wall space for the hanging and cut the background fabric to size, allowing extra for turnings. Roughly mark out the basic plan on the fabric using felt pen.

3. Cut a piece of green fabric for the foreground and glue into position. Cut a piece of blue fabric for the sea and glue that into position also. Paint the sky area or use fabric.

4. Ask one group of children to cut stone shapes out of grey fabrics and glue into position for the wall.

5. Using felt pen, draw the outline of the tree canopy on a piece of loose-weave hessian. Cut double leaf shapes out of green plastic bags and, using the point of a pencil, poke both ends of the leaf shape through the hessian. When no hessian is visible through the leaves, glue the canopy into position.

6. For the grass, cut 25cm squares of hessian. Rule a ruler-width margin all the way around each square with felt pen. Diagonally cut strips of green fabric 2–3cm wide and 8–10cm long. Using a pencil, poke both ends of the strips through the hessian to form a tufty texture. Work in rows, keeping within the margins to prevent fraying. Glue the finished squares along the bottom edge of the picture.

7. Make the tree trunk by twisting lengths of stick weaving together. Thread the weaving sticks with the appropriate length warp threads and weave in and out of the sticks until reaching the top. Then gently twist and pull each stick upwards and the weaving will pass down onto the warp threads.

8. Cut a snake shape from suitable fabric; sew and stuff. Intertwine with the stick weaving. Glue into position.

9. For the figures, draw simple head, body, arm and leg shapes. Cut a front and a back for each body part; sew together and stuff. With supervision, older children should be able to use a sewing machine to sew the long seams on these parts. Hand sew the parts together. Sew on fur fabric or wool for hair. Add felt features. For tunics, cut long rectangles of fabric, cut a head hole in the centre and pass over the doll's head. Tie in place with a belt. Glue the figures onto the picture.

10. Make simple flower shapes from scraps of felt and glue along the base of the wall. Add the boat and the harpies.

Perseus the Gorgon Slayer

Approach

1. Read the story together as a class and decide which scene to illustrate on the hanging.

2. Cut a piece of blue fabric to size. Glue a piece of green fabric onto this to create the hills. To make a foreground, glue down stone shapes cut from grey fabrics.

3. Make three-dimensional stones by sewing two shapes together and stuffing. Glue these to form a mound.

4. Medusa's hair is made from lengths of French knitting but lengths of cord could be used instead.

5. To make the head, simply stuff a length of old tights. Use several lengths of tights fabric together for strength. Sew on the eyes and tongue made from felt.

6. To create the wings, cut scale shapes from shiny fabric and glue to the wing shapes cut from interfacing.

7. Cut Medusa's body parts from scaly patterned fabric, sew and stuff.

8. Cut an invisible Perseus from clear polythene and make his shield from card covered with kitchen foil.

9. Glue Medusa and Perseus to the display.

Resources
- Fabrics of various colours (blue, green and grey)
- Clear polythene
- Card
- Lengths of cord
- Kitchen foil
- Latex fabric glue
- Old tights
- Shiny fabric
- Sewing machine
- Interfacing

Fabric Containers

Rag Weaving

Resources
- A selection of plain and patterned fabric (old T-shirts, sweat shirts, sheets, curtains, dresses)
- A simple nail frame
- Strong thread
- Large button or clasp
- Latex fabric glue
- Braid, cord or rope

Approach

1. A nail frame can be made from an old wooden picture frame. Simply knock in panel pins or small nails at 1cm intervals top and bottom. Warp up the loom with strong coloured thread.

2. Cut long strips of fabric. Thicker fabrics need to be quite narrow (about 1.5cm). Thinner fabrics, such as chiffon or voile, can be 3 or 4cm or even wider.

3. Weave several rows in one colour. Always join new strips at a point near the middle of the weaving and not at the end of the row. Joining at the end makes the edges weak and untidy. Push the end of the strip to the back of the work, count back three or four warp threads and join the new length at this point, repeating the under/over pattern of the previous row. Once past the join, the pattern will be correct.

4. Take care not to pull the strips tightly at the edges of the work or the weaving will narrow. To prevent narrowing, the warp threads at each side of the work can be tied to the wooden frame to keep them parallel.

5. Beat the weaving down well every few rows (a large comb with a handle is useful for this).

6. When the work is complete, slip the warp threads off the nails. Ease the weaving up against the end loops, thus ensuring a firm edge.

7. Cut off all ends from the back of the work. If the weaving is tight and firm, the ends will not work loose.

8. Fold the bottom section of the work up and glue the sides together (using latex fabric glue) to form a bag. Leave a section at the top that can be folded down to create a flap.

9. To disguise the side seams, make a long plait from strips of fabric. Make it long enough to cover both side seams and form a handle. Glue into position. Use the glue sparingly.

10. Finish with a button or clasp. The button can be pushed through the weave of the fabric and fastened with a loop.

Heart Shaped Woven Bag

Resources
- Imitation leather/vinyl fabric or sticky-backed plastic
- Iron-on interfacing
- Plain and patterned fabrics

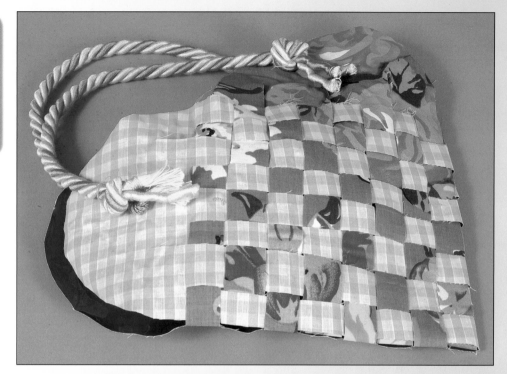

Approach

1. From card, cut a rectangle twice as long as it is wide. Trim the top edge to a curve.

2. Use this as a template to cut two fabric shapes each from a different colour or one patterned and one plain. To do this, fold the fabric and place the short straight edge of the template on the fold. Draw around the template and cut out. Repeat with interfacing if using this. Bond the interfacing to the fabric.

3. Cut slits in the folded edges of the shapes, cutting upwards for the measurement of the folded edge plus 2cm. You may wish to cut four, six, eight or more strips depending upon the size of the bag or the ability of the children.

4. Place the two folded shapes at right angles to each other on the worktop, straight edges nearest.

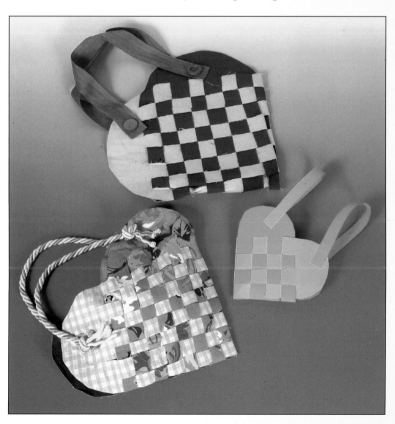

5. Take the first strip of 'H' (horizontal shape) and push this through the first folded strip of 'V' (vertical shape). Next take the second strip of 'V' and push it through the first strip of 'H'. Take the first strip of 'H' and push it through the third strip of 'V'. Take the fourth strip of 'V' and push it through the first strip of 'H'. Continue along the row in this fashion until the first row of strips is interlocked. Push this row up to the top of the slits.

6. Take the first strip of 'V' and push this through the second strip of 'H'. Take the second strip of 'H' and push this through the second strip of 'V'. Take the third strip of 'V' and push this through the second strip of 'H'. Take the second strip of 'H' and push this through the fourth strip of 'V'. Continue along the row in this fashion until all the strips are interlocked.

7. Repeat this two-row pattern until all the strips are interlocked. The shapes should now open up to form a bag. For extra strength, put spots of glue under the weave.

8. Add handles made from fabric strips, cord, braid or rope.

Mixed Media Wall Hangings

Nursery Rhyme/Fairy Tale Cottage

This wall hanging was inspired by popular nursery rhymes and stories. There are many stories and rhymes that could be used as a starting point for a similar project.

Resources

- Old white sheet or poly cotton sheeting for background fabric
- Selection of green fabrics
- Loosely woven hessian
- Green plastic bags
- Fabrics in flower colours
- Thin purple fabric
- Toy filler
- Pale coloured poly cotton for curtains
- Round objects for printing, such as cotton reels, corks, card tubing and bottle tops
- Brightly coloured ready-mixed paints
- Small squared (about 1cm) plastic garden mesh
- Strips of brown fabric for window frames
- Green velvet for field
- Scraps of patterned fabric
- Peg looms
- Assorted wools
- Latex fabric glue
- Felt pen

Approach

1. Decide where the panel is going to hang and cut the background fabric accordingly, allowing extra for turnings around the edges. The hanging can be as large or small as you wish depending upon the amount of time available and the size of the group – class, year group or school.

2. Mark out a large area for the window using a felt pen. Using ready-mixed paint, paint the rest of the cloth white or a pastel colour. This will stiffen the cloth as well as creating the impression of the cottage wall.

3. Glue a length of patterned fabric across half of the window space as 'wallpaper'. Draw a smaller window on this.

4. To make the curtains, cut lengths of pale cotton to fit the large 'window', remembering to allow a little extra for turning and gathering around the edges. Print all over this using brightly coloured ready-mixed paints and an assortment of round objects. Cut fabric to fit the smaller 'window'. Print on this using smaller objects such as off-cuts of dowel and corks.

5. Create a scene in the smaller window using blue cotton for the sky and green velvet for the hill. Add a well and Jack and Jill made from fabric.

6. Gather up the curtains and glue into position, turning under the raw edges as you go.

Leaves Cut 12cm squares of hessian. Cut double leaf shapes from green plastic bags. Make a hole in the centre of the hessian with a pencil point; poke one end of the leaf shape through, make another hole and poke the other end of the leaf shape through, so that both leaves are on the same side of the fabric. Repeat this, filling in from the centre outwards. Poke the leaves in close together so that the hessian doesn't show on the right side. Make lots of these tufts. Trim off excess hessian and glue along the top edge of the picture.

Plums Cut saucer sized circles of thin purple fabric. Sew around the circumference with running stitch. Draw up to form a little bag. Stuff with toy filler and sew up the opening. Glue the plums between the leaves.

Grass Cut 10cm squares of plastic mesh. Have prepared lots of green clippings about 12cm long and 2cm wide, cut diagonally to form points. Poke one end of a piece of fabric through a hole in the mesh and then poke the other end through the next hole so that both ends are on the same side of the mesh. Fill in the whole square. Glue the completed squares along the bottom edge of the picture.

Mesh Flowers Proceed as above but use flower coloured fabric on circular pieces of mesh (trim the corners off the 10cm squares). When the mesh is full, cut out a small circle of coloured felt, separate the 'petals' and glue the flower centre into position.

Flowers on Hessian Glue a circle of felt in the centre of a square of hessian. On the back of the hessian, mark the edge of the circle with felt pen to provide a guideline for pegging. Cut petals as for grass but in bright colours. Poke through as for the leaves, working around the guideline. One ring of petals is sufficient but two looks better. A ring of green sepals could also be worked.

Plant Leaves Cut card templates of leaf shapes or let the children make their own patterns. Draw round the templates on green fabrics and cut out. Mark in veins with felt pen. Cut strips of fabric for stems. Glue down flowers, stems and leaves.

Ladder Prepare tubes of thin brown fabric for the rungs and sides of the ladder. Let the children stuff these with toy filler. Glue onto the background to form the ladder.

Patchwork Mat Use peg looms (available from certain school suppliers) to weave small rectangles of brightly coloured weaving. Glue these into the bottom part of the window space to create a mat on the room floor. Fill in any extra space with neutrally coloured fabric.

Finishing Off Glue strips of brown fabric around the windows. Cut out a table from brown fabric. Add Baby Bunting in his cradle under the table. Cut three simple bear faces from fur fabric. Glue to one side, peeping from behind the curtains. Add simple furniture and Cinderella. Use a piece of patterned fabric for Mother Hubbard's bottom. Pad lightly and glue to the hanging. Add Tom Thumb's face peeping out of the leaves at the top of the ladder.

The Four Seasons

Resources

- Pale blue cotton background fabric
- Loosely woven hessian
- Felts in all colours
- Green plastic bags
- Thick embroidery threads
- Iron-on interfacing
- String
- Raffia
- Brown and pink wools
- Beads
- White and silver/icy fabrics
- Wadding
- Thin green fabric
- Toy filler
- Weaving sticks or fat drinking straws
- French knitting bobbins
- Latex fabric glue

Approach

Tree Trunk Thread up the weaving sticks as per manufacturer's instructions and use in fours. If these are not available, use fat drinking straws and pass the warp thread through the straw. Knot both ends of the warp thread together and pull the knot to the bottom. Weave long strips in bark colours. Cut off the straws when the weaving is finished.

French Knitting Knit lengths in bark colours to twist with the weaving and others in green to make stems for ivy. If neither of the above is available, sew tubes of brown fabric and stuff lightly with toy filler. Twist together to create gnarled trunk and branches. Glue into position.

Spring Blossom Finger knit pink knitting wool of various shades. Thicker wool grows more quickly but if using thin wools, finger knit the lengths of finished finger knitting several times until it becomes chunky. To finger knit, tie a loop in the end of the wool several centimetres from the end. Do not cut the wool off the ball. Put the loop on the index finger. Hold the short end of wool just below the knot with the thumb and second finger. With the other hand, pass the long length of wool over the index finger towards the front. Hold this with the finger and thumb whilst passing the first loop over the second. Pull on the long end to reduce the size of the stitch. Repeat. Scrunch up the finished lengths and glue down to look like blossom.

Summer Leaves Cut 15cm squares of hessian. Cut double leaf shapes from plastic bags and proceed as instructed for **Leaves** on page 61.

Birds Make a simple bird template. Cut out a back and front from felt, stitch and stuff. Add slightly padded wings.

Nests Cut a nest pattern, ensuring that the bird will fit in. Cut the nest from hessian and back with iron-on interfacing. This stops the hessian from falling apart while sewing. Create texture by attaching on lengths of string, raffia and wool.

Apples Cut circles of thin green fabric and proceed as for **Plums** on page 61. Streak some of the apples with yellow and red felt pen.

Autumn Leaves Draw various leaf shapes on paper, cut out and use as patterns for cutting felt leaves in autumn colours. Decorate with stitching and beads.

Grass Cut 30cm squares of hessian. Draw a ruler width margin all the way around the square. Work within this marked area to prevent fraying. Cut pieces of green fabric approximately 10cm by 2cm. Following one side of the margin, make a hole with a pencil point and poke one end of a piece of fabric through the hole. Make another hole very close to the first hole and poke the other end of the green fabric through. Pull both ends level. Continue in this way, working from the back of the fabric. Work in rows close together. Trim off any excess hessian before gluing into place.

Winter Snows Cut rectangles of white cotton. On top of the cotton, place a piece of thin wadding. On top of this, place a piece of white satin. Pin and tack together through all layers. To this, sew snippets of sparkling, icy materials, silver sequins, shiny plastics, bubble wrap and so on. Cut a piece of white backing fabric the size of the winter section of the hanging and collage together the smaller sections. If possible, sew across this several times with a sewing machine to obliterate the joins.

Hedgehogs Make pompoms by winding on several shades of brown wool at a time. Cut two headpieces from felt; sew around the two long sides and stuff with toy filler. Using latex glue, stick the head to the pompom, pressing it well into the cut threads. Glue on felt eyes.

Squirrels Make a simple head and body template. Use to cut out two felt shapes. Sew together around the edges, leaving a gap for stuffing. Stuff with toy filler and sew up the gap. Make a template for the large back legs and another for the arms. Cut four of each from felt and sew together in pairs, stuffing lightly. Sew the limbs to the squirrel.

Ivy Cut small leaves from green felt and sew to lengths of green French knitting or finger knitting. Glue into position on the tree trunk.

Assemble as illustrated. Use a piece of green velvet for the background to the spring section. Cut spring flowers from felt. Add butterflies from printed fabric.

Slippers

Approach

1. Ask the children to describe or bring into school their favourite slippers. Have available various styles of slipper, such as mule, moccasin, sheepskin, themed slipper and traditional slipper. Identify the various parts of the slipper: sole, upper and inner lining and cushion. Consider who might wear which kind of slipper.

2. Work out how the slipper is constructed by first making a maquette (small preliminary model) from paper and card. Ask the children to make this to fit their own foot.

3. Next, ask them to design a slipper for a certain market: small child, teenager, adult and so on. Start by drawing around a suitably sized foot. Adjust the shape and allow extra for comfort. Cut the sole from carton card. They may wish to glue two layers of card together.

4. Cut another sole shape from thin sheet foam and glue this to the card. Cut a sole lining from felt or fleece. Glue on top of the foam. Use the glue sparingly.

5. Cut a strip of fabric long enough to extend all the way around the edge of the card sole plus 1cm, and deep enough to cover the side of the foot plus 4cm for turning. From fabric, cut a 'U' shape the size of the top of the foot, allowing 1cm all the way round for turnings.

6. Turn under and sew the short straight edge of the 'U' shaped piece of fabric. Fold the long strip in half to find the centre point and with right sides together, pin the centre point of the strip to the centre of the curve of the 'U'. Pin the rest of the strip around the curved sides of the 'U'. Sew securely.

7. Spread fabric glue around the edge of the toe end of the slipper and carefully position the fabric upper centrally onto the card edge, allowing 2cm for turning under the sole. Hold in position until the glue sets. Gluing a little at a time, gradually attach the upper all the way around the sole. Glue or stitch the back seam. Glue the overlap to the underside of the sole, snipping to ease around the curve.

8. Cut out a fabric or imitation leather sole and glue over the overlap.

Mules

Make in the same way as the basic slipper but only extend the long strip halfway along the foot or to the depth of the 'U' shape. Glue braid to the exposed card edge. If desired, add elastic to extend around the heel.

Themed Slippers

Vehicles

1. Cut a 'windscreen' from white felt the same width as the short edge of the 'U'. Stiffen with iron-on interfacing and sew to the 'U'. If desired, add 'eyes'. Cut wheels from felt, stiffen and glue to the sides of the slipper.

2. Alternatively, cut out the motif of a vehicle and glue to the top of the slipper.

Tractor Slipper

1. Cut a rectangle of card for the sole. Pad and line as before.

2. Cut a piece of fabric the width of the rectangle and long enough to extend above the ankle. Remember to add extra for sewing and turning under the sole. Cut two more pieces the same size as this. Sew these together so that they fit around the back part of the slipper. This is part of the tractor 'cab'. Do not glue yet.

3. Remembering to add extra for turnings, cut two narrower side pieces and sew these to the sides of the 'cab'.

4. Cut a piece to fit all the way up the front of the tractor to the top of the cab. Sew into place.

5. Carefully glue the sole into position. Complete as for the basic slipper.

6. Glue on a piece of white felt for the windscreen and black felt wheels.

Purses, Wallets and Bags

Resources

- Brightly coloured cottons
- Fur fabric
- Felt
- Furnishing fabrics, satin, vinyl or imitation leather, iron-on interfacing
- Metal clasps
- Press studs
- Hooks and eyes, buttons, zips
- Self-adhesive Velcro
- Beads, sequins, fringing, braid
- Bias binding
- Sewing threads
- Electric sewing machine if available
- An iron
- Examples of commercially produced purses and bags

Approach

Ask the children to examine commercially produced purses, looking carefully at the ways in which they are constructed and fastened. Take particular note of gussets, pockets and folds. Consider linings. At what stage of the sewing process should they be included? Practise ways of folding with sheets of A4 and A3 paper. Develop a plan and then a full sized pattern of the purse.

Simple Imitation Leather Purse with Clasp

1. Cut a rectangle of vinyl 24cm by 12cm. Fold over 9cm with right side facing. Use blanket stitch and strong thread to fasten the sides together. Fasten off securely. If the vinyl is particularly hard, pierce a row of holes with a large needle before attempting to sew.

2. Position half of the clasp on the purse flap and sew. Fold down the flap and position the other half of the clasp. Sew.

Gusseted, Lined Wallet with Pockets

1. From furnishing fabric, cut a rectangle 30cm by 42cm. Cut another from thin lining fabric. Sew these two pieces together all the way round, leaving a small opening through which to turn the fabric to the right side. Turn and sew up the opening.

2. Cut two pieces of fabric 16cm by 13cm. Hem the top of each and turn under the remaining sides to create a pocket piece 11cm square.

3. Cut two more pieces 12cm by 11cm, hem and turn under to make pockets 8cm square. Sew the smaller pocket pieces to the larger ones.

4. Now position the double pockets in the top left and right hand corners of the large rectangle on the right side of the fabric. Sew into position, remembering to leave the top edge of the pocket open!

5. Fold the large rectangle in half, thus making an open wallet shape. To make gussets for the ends of the wallet, cut rectangles of felt 3cm by 12cm. Sew into position at each end between the folded halves of the large rectangle.

6. Sew through the folded wallet in two places to create three equal pockets.

7. Fold the wallet up to position the fasteners (press studs, hooks and eyes or Velcro).

Lined Drawstring Bag

1. Cut two rectangles of fabric (one patterned, one plain) for the bag and the lining.

2. Take the patterned rectangle and fold it in half with the right sides together. Sew around three sides. Repeat with the lining.

3. Turn the patterned bag the right way out and place the lining bag inside the other so that the raw edges are hidden between the layers.

4. Turn in the top edges of both bags to create a neat edge. Sew.

5. Make a slot by sewing around the bag 3cm below the top edge. Snip a hole in the lining for the drawstring. Alternatively, sew a strip of coloured tape around the bag 3cm below the top edge, leaving gaps at each side for the drawstring. Finish off with one or two drawstrings as preferred.

Black Fur Heart Shaped Bag

Approach

1. Draw a truncated heart shape on paper, cut out and use this as a pattern to cut out a back and a front from fur fabric.

2. Cut two small rectangles of smooth, thin cotton, hem and sew to the wrong side of each fur fabric piece for inside pockets.

3. Put the bag pieces together, fur to the inside, and sew around the straight edges. Turn the right way out and blanket stitch around the curved edges in a contrasting thread.

4. Cut out and glue a contrasting coloured furry motif to the front of the bag and decorate with sequins.

5. Sew hooks and eyes to the top edges of the bag to fasten. Attach a length of silk cord for a handle.

Pink Fur Fabric Rectangular Bag

Approach

1. Cut out a rectangle from fur fabric. Turn up a little more than $\frac{2}{3}$ of the rectangle so that the wrong side of the fabric is on the outside. Sew the sides and turn the purse the right way out. Neaten the remaining edges.

2. Sew a length of gathered broderie anglaise to the top edge of the purse and lengths of sequin trim to the front.

3. Sew on large press studs to fasten and a length of braid or cord for a handle.

Switch and Circuit Models

Camping Lanterns

Before starting the activity, allow the children to practise making simple circuits. Also, take a look at some commercially produced lanterns for design ideas.

Resources
- Bulbs
- Bulb holders
- Cells
- Clear packaging plastic
- Cheese box with lid
- Card
- Plastic-coated electrical wire
- Paper clips
- Drawing pins
- Card
- Masking tape
- A selection of reclaimed materials
- Reflective materials
- Wood off-cuts and tools, such as small screwdrivers, wire strippers and cutters

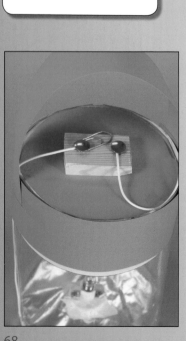

Approach

1. Cut a strip of card and glue around the cheese box base to make it deeper so that it will house the battery.

2. Cut two lengths of wire and connect to the bulb holder. Tape the bulb holder to the cheese box base, pierce two holes in the base and pass the wires through to the underside.

3. Tape the cell to the underside of the base. Connect one of the wires to the cell using a paper clip or tape.

4. Cover the base in reflective material such as baking foil.

5. Use clear packaging plastic to make a tube for the lantern casing. Screw the bulb into the bulb holder and slip the casing over the base. Tape in place using clear tape.

6. Cut another length of wire and attach to the other cell terminal.

7. Run the remaining wires from the bulb and cell up the sides of the lantern casing and tape in place. Tape the cheese box lid into the top of the casing. Glue a short off-cut of wood to the lid.

8. Make a simple switch from drawing pins, paper clip and the wood off-cut as illustrated, connect up and switch on!

9. Cut a strip of card and glue in place as a handle.

Vehicle with Headlights

Approach

1. Cut holes in both ends of the shoebox large enough to accommodate the top of the bulb holders. Connect two of the holders together with a length of flex. Repeat for the rear lights.

2. Cut two pieces of flex a little longer than the shoebox. Connect these to the first pair of bulb holders. Push the bulb holders through the holes at the front of the box from the inside. Tape the bases securely to the inside of the box.

3. Run the long wires to the back of the box and tape to the sides. Connect one wire to one of the rear bulb holders. Connect the other wire to a crocodile connector.

4. Cut another length of flex and connect to the fourth bulb holder. Pierce a hole in the base of the box and push the other end of the wire through.

5. Make a simple switch (as described on page 68) and glue to the upturned box. Connect the wire to one of the drawing pins. Cut another length of flex, attach to the other drawing pin and push through to the underside of the box. Attach a crocodile connector.

6. Tape the battery to the underside of the box, screw in all the light bulbs, connect up to the battery and switch on! Because this is a series circuit, the lights will be dim. Try connecting as a parallel circuit and note the difference. Try using an extra battery as well.

7. Complete the vehicle as described on pages 10 to 11.

Resources
- Shoebox with lid
- Small box
- 4 bulb holders with bulbs
- Flex
- 4.5-volt 'flat' cell
- Drawing pins
- Paper clip
- Small wood off-cut
- Masking tape
- Crocodile connectors

Buzzer Tile

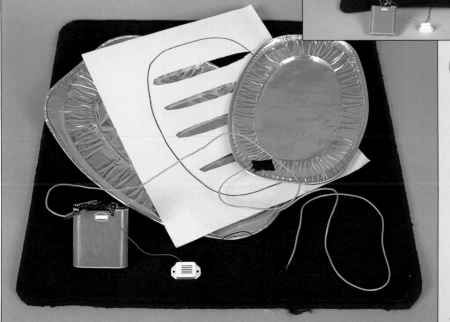

Resources
- 2 foil plates
- Card
- Wire
- Cell
- Buzzer
- Carpet tile
- Crocodile connectors

Approach

1. Cut two lengths of wire. Attach crocodile connectors to three of the ends. Clip a connector to each of the foil plates.

2. Cut a piece of card larger than the plates. Cut 1–2cm wide slits in the piece of card. Sandwich the card between the plates. Place the carpet tile over the plates.

3. Connect one length of wire to the cell and attach the other to the buzzer. Attach the buzzer to the cell.

4. Stand on the carpet tile and the alarm will buzz!

69

Models with Motors

Aerofoil

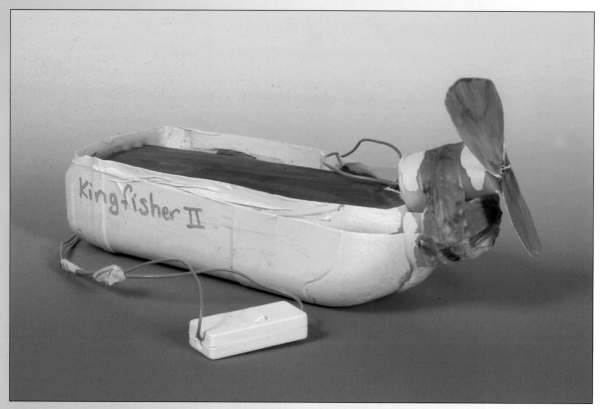

Approach

1. Cut the plastic bottle vertically in half. Place one half inside the other for strength and tape together.

2. Pierce a hole in the lid and base of one of the film cases. Cut two lengths of flex, one the length of the boat and the other much longer, and wire to the motor. Put the motor into the film case with the spindle poking through the hole in the bottom of the case. Push the two lengths of flex through the hole in the lid. Fasten the lid.

3. Tape a small piece of wood into the neck of the bottle. Mount the film case containing the motor onto this, securing with elastic bands and tape. The use of film cases to house both battery and motor is to ensure that they do not come into contact with the water.

4. Cut a propeller from packaging plastic and push onto the spindle. Connect the long wire from the motor to the switch. Connect the shorter wire to the battery using electrical tape. Cut another long length of flex and tape to the other battery terminal. Put the battery into the other film case, make a hole in the lid and push the wires through. Fasten the lid.

5. Secure the film case to a short length of wood with elastic bands and tape the wood into the bottom of the boat for stability.

6. Connect the remaining wire to the switch. Reassemble the switch and check that the propeller rotates when the switch is operated. Float the boat and watch it move! First ask the children which way they think it will go. They may be surprised!

Resources
- Large plastic bottle, e.g. 2-litre milk bottle
- Photography film cases
- Scraps of wood
- Elastic bands
- Packaging plastic
- Wire
- Cylindrical battery
- Switch
- Motor
- Masking tape
- Electrical tape
- Cell

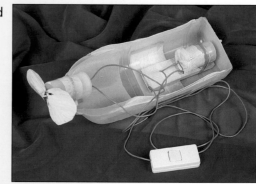

Motorised Chassis

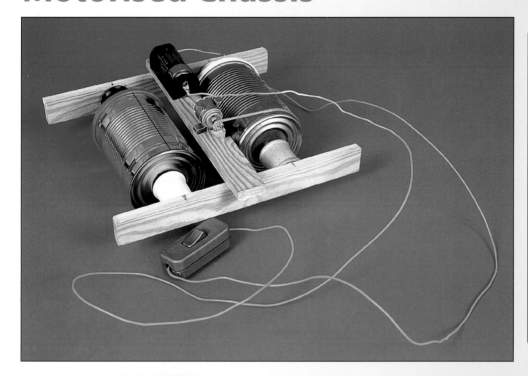

Resources
- Wood off-cuts
- Tin cans, each with one end safely removed
- Plastic tin can lids (cat food covers)
- Cotton reels
- Dowel
- Elastic bands
- Motor
- Cell
- Cell holder
- Wire
- Switch
- 2 terry clips
- Reclaimed packaging materials
- Card
- Beads

Approach

1. Pierce a hole centrally in the bottom of each can large enough to accommodate the dowel. Pierce same sized holes in the plastic lids. Cut two 19cm lengths of dowel for the axles and thread onto each a tin can and two cotton reels, placing the cotton reels either side of the can.

2. Cut two lengths of wood for the sides of the chassis. Using a hand drill, drill holes in these to receive the ends of the axles. Before fixing the axles into place, slip a strong elastic band onto one of the cans. This will be the drive belt.

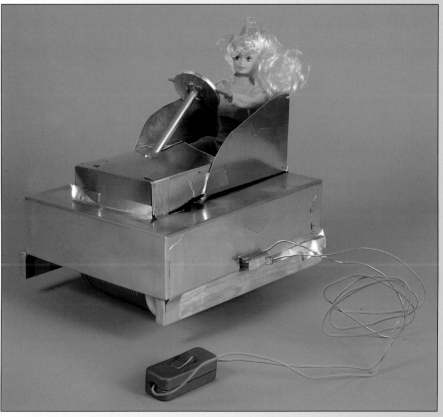

3. Cut another length of wood the width of the chassis and fasten the motor to this using a terry clip. Glue this piece of wood to the chassis between the cans, first checking that the elastic band clears the edge of the wood when it is stretched around the motor spindle. If it does not, cut a section out of the wood at this point. Glue a small bead to the end of the spindle to prevent the band from slipping off.

4. Fasten the cell holder to the wood behind the motor and insert the cell. Wire up the motor, cell and switch.

5. Complete the vehicle using reclaimed materials and card. Decorate as desired.

Powered Carousel

Resources

- Small strong cardboard box with lid
- Cotton reel
- Dowel
- Elastic band
- Small bead
- Egg box
- Strong thread
- Card or circular card lid
- Metal washers
- Masking tape
- Motor
- Cell
- Wire
- Switch

Approach

1. Cut two short lengths of wire and attach them to the motor. Fasten the motor vertically to the inside of the box, making sure that the spindle is clear of the lid of the box when closed.

2. Glue a cotton reel to the base of the box. Make a hole in the box lid above the hole in the reel.

3. Cut a length of dowel for the carousel support and put it into the hole in the cotton reel.

4. Stretch an elastic band over the dowel and the motor spindle. Push a small bead onto the end of the spindle to prevent the band from slipping.

5. Tape the cell to the inside of the box. Connect the cell to the motor.

6. Pierce a hole in the side of the box and push the remaining wire through to the outside. Connect this to the switch. Cut another length of wire, push one end through the hole and attach the switch to the cell. Fasten the switch to the outside of the box.

7. Put the lid on the box so that only the carousel support is visible. Make the carousel top from a circular box lid or card. Cut sections of egg box for seats and suspend from the lid. Weight the seats with metal washers or play dough so that they hang correctly.

8. Make a hole in the centre of the lid and press it onto the dowel. Secure with glue. Press the switch and the carousel will turn. Create a domed top for the carousel by the addition of an upturned yoghurt pot. Paint using bright colours.